CULTURES OF THE WORLD

GUATEMALA

Sean Sheehan

MARSHALL CAVENDISH
New York • London • Sydney

Reference edition published 1998 by
Marshall Cavendish Corporation
99 White Plains Road
Tarrytown
New York 10591

© Times Editions Pte Ltd 1998

Originated and designed by
Times Books International, an imprint of
Times Editions Pte Ltd

Printed in Singapore

Library of Congress Cataloging-in-Publication Data:

Sheehan, Sean, 1951–
       Guatemala / Sean Sheehan.
          p. cm.—(Cultures of the World)
       Includes bibliographical references and index.
       Summary: Introduces the geography, history, religion,
government, economy, and culture of one of the poorest
countries in the western hemisphere.
       ISBN 0-7614-0812-6 (lib. bdg.)
       1. Guatemala—Juvenile literature. [1. Guatemala]
I. Title. II. Series.
F1463.2.S5   1998
972.81—dc21   97–44619
                                     CIP
                                     AC

INTRODUCTION

GUATEMALA IS A SCENIC LANDSCAPE of smoldering volcanoes and swirling mists, where the tropical hues of nature complement the rainbow colors of traditional dress. It is also a land of grueling poverty. One of the poorest countries in the Western Hemisphere, Guatemala suffers from an uneven distribution of wealth and opportunities for its people.

Guatemalans, however, are living heirs to the ancient Mayas, and the creative spirit that sustained the sophisticated Mayan civilization has become part of the country's rich potential. Now that peace has finally come, after the longest civil war anywhere in the Americas, Guatemala is on the brink of a new era of reconciliation and development. As the next century approaches, this vibrant and brave Central American country is embarking on a new chapter in its history.

CONTENTS

Handwoven masks for sale at a Guatemalan market.

CONTENTS

Bright colors and embroidery characterize Guatemalan handicrafts.

GEOGRAPHY

GUATEMALA IS THE THIRD LARGEST country in Central America and is about the same size as Ireland or Ohio. It shares a border to the north and west with Mexico, and one with Belize on the northeast. Honduras lies to Guatemala's east and El Salvador to its southeast. The Caribbean forms only a short coastline in the northeast, but the southern coast of the Pacific Ocean stretches for 150 miles (240 km).

Guatemala has three main geographic regions: highlands, lowlands, and a coastal plain. The volcanic uplands that form the southern half of the highlands join the coastal plain in a downward slope toward the Pacific. Within these two areas—the volcanic uplands and the coastal plain—reside about 60% of the population. Most of the remaining 40% live in the mountains to the north of the volcanic uplands. The country as a whole has a very high population density, higher than that of any other Latin American country.

The 1976 earthquake affected 8% of Guatemala's territory, killing about 30,000 people and rendering about 20% of the population homeless.

Opposite and left: **Located in a region of frequent seismic and volcanic activity, Guatemala has some of the world's most scenic landscapes. High mountains and deep, broad volcanic lakes provide a splendid backdrop for the active volcanoes in the country.**

Guatemala's lakes provide an ideal environment for boating. Lake Atitlán, in the highlands, reaches depths of more than 1,000 feet (305 m).

HIGHLANDS

The highlands of Guatemala, land that lies above 1,000 feet (305 m), make up about half of the country's total land area. They cut across the middle of Guatemala, from the southeast to the northwest, for a distance of 180 miles (290 km). The southern range of mountains, the Sierra Madre, includes over 30 volcanic peaks stretching down from southern Mexico. They include the country's highest mountain, Tajumulco, at 13,845 feet (4,218 m). Some of the volcanoes are active and some are dormant. Major earthquakes occurred in 1717, 1773, 1917, and 1976.

Two major rivers separate the southern volcanic landscape from other mountains, or sierras, to the north. One of the rivers, Motagua, flows toward the Caribbean, while the other, Cuilco, flows west. Rivers in the northern region tend to flow north into the Gulf of Mexico. There are two large lakes on the southern side of the highlands, Lake Atitlán and Lake Amatitlán.

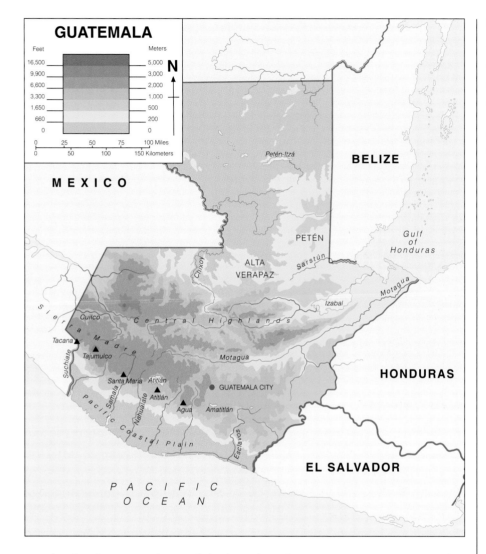

GUATEMALA

Feet	Meters
16,500	5,000
9,900	3,000
6,600	2,000
3,300	1,000
1,650	500
660	200
0	0

0   25   50   75   100 Miles
0   50   100   150 Kilometers

N

MEXICO

BELIZE

Petén-Itzá

PETÉN

Gulf of Honduras

Chixoy

ALTA VERAPAZ

Sarstún

Motagua

Izabal

Sierra Madre

Quilco

Central Highlands

Tacana

Tajumulco

Motagua

Santa María   Atitlán

HONDURAS

Atitlán

GUATEMALA CITY

Suchiate

Samalá

Nahualate

Agua   Amatitlán

Pacific Coastal Plain

Esclavos

EL SALVADOR

PACIFIC OCEAN

Guatemala's history, like its geography, is greatly influenced by the number of earthquakes it experiences. The Sierra Madre includes 33 volcanic peaks, many of which are still active.

The land is very beautiful, dotted with ancient Mayan towns that proudly preserve the Indian culture. Notwithstanding the very real threat of another earthquake, most people here are farmers, growing corn and vegetables in the valleys in a manner not very different from the way their pre-Columbian ancestors did.

Most of Guatemala's cities and towns are situated in the southern half of the country. Apart from a few coastal settlements, the highlands are the most populated area of the country.

Guatemala still retains a vast expanse of natural rainforest, but the rapidly increasing population leads to more and more tracts of land being cleared for agriculture.

LOWLANDS

The Petén lowlands, with an elevation between 500 and 700 feet (150 and 200 m), form part of a fairly level limestone shelf that includes Yucatán in Mexico. Limestone is easy to cut and makes an ideal plaster, properties that were artistically exploited by the Maya, who made Petén the heartland of their civilization. Some of the most spectacular ancient Mayan cities are in this region, although many more probably remain undiscovered and buried in the jungle, because the region is mostly covered with thick rainforests and broad swamps. Caves are easily formed in limestone regions and the Maya treated them as holy places. This is vividly depicted in murals and texts found in the Naj Tanuch Cave, which was only discovered in 1980. Yet another consequence of the limestone landscape is the relative absence of rivers because most of the rainfall is drained underground through the porous limestone.

The area takes up about one-third of the country's land but only about 2% of the population live here because it is not well suited to agriculture.

This has not stopped people from moving to Petén and using slash-and-burn agriculture in an attempt to make a living from farming. Although about 90% of Petén is still covered with primary forest, this figure will steadily decline if slash-and-burn agriculture continues.

The isolation and low population help explain the rich wildlife in Petén. There are over 300 species of birds alone. The economic value of Petén lies in its forests of mahogany, rubber, and tropical cedar. The main town is Flores, and the land around it is cultivated for sugarcane and fruit. The town lies on Lake Petén-Itzá, an Indian area that was not conquered by the Spanish until the end of the 17th century.

COASTAL PLAIN

Guatemala's Pacific littoral (a region lying along a shore) is where the volcanic slopes drop close to the sea, forming a beach of black volcanic sand. The area is characterized by mangrove swamps and rich alluvial soil that nourishes a fertile plain up to 45 miles (72 km) wide and 150 miles (240 km) long. Grass grows easily here and cattle ranches thrive alongside plantations of coffee, sugar, cacao, cotton, soya, sorghum, and fruit. The capital and other big cities are situated on this plain, despite the constant threat of earthquakes and volcanic eruptions.

The area also includes the largest lake in the country, Lake Izabal. The sea supports a small fishing industry in tuna, shrimp, and mackerel, and the sandy shore attracts sea turtles in search of nests for their eggs.

CLIMATE

Although Guatemala lies in the tropics, there is a diversity of climate, depending on regional elevation and proximity to the coast. From sea level to around 6,000 feet (1,830 m) temperatures range between 77°F and 86°F (25°C and 30°C) during the day, with nights being chilly but not terribly cold. Most of the country's major towns are located within these altitudes. However, the daytime temperature drops to as low as 52°F (11°C) when the land rises to over 7,000 feet (2,135 m), and at night the temperature plunges to freezing in the highlands. The lowlands are hot and steamy, with heavy rain in the summer but little during the dry season.

The months between November and April are generally the driest in Guatemala, but both the Pacific and the Caribbean coastal areas remain humid and rainy throughout the year. Rainfall varies from 80 inches (203 cm) in the highlands to less than half that in the driest season. Tropical storms sometimes occur during the months of September and October.

The main advantage of the country's varied climate is that virtually every crop that can be grown in the Western Hemisphere can be cultivated somewhere in Guatemala.

Opposite: **Guatemala City, the capital of Guatemala and center of business and trade.**

CITIES

The capital of Guatemala used to be Antigua but an earthquake in 1773 virtually destroyed the town, so a new capital, Guatemala City, was founded three years later in a neighboring highland valley. The new capital was not immune to natural disasters; a series of destructive earthquakes struck in 1917 and 1918. Rather than establish another new capital, it was decided that the town should be rebuilt. Today about one in five Guatemalans live in the capital, accounting for half the country's urban population and making Guatemala City the largest city in Central America.

Guatemala City is the capital of the country in economic, political, and cultural terms, and it continues to grow and dominate many aspects of national life. It is not an especially attractive city nor does it have the cultural history of some other Guatemalan cities. While there are glistening skyscrapers in the city center, the majority of people experience a low standard of living and occupy poor shanty dwellings.

The second largest city in Guatemala is Quezaltenango, also in the highlands but some distance west of the capital. It grew prosperous during the 19th century because of world demand for coffee, but an earthquake in 1902 destroyed it. Although it was rebuilt, many families moved to Guatemala City. Compared to the capital, Quezaltenango has a provincial atmosphere but is generally regarded as more interesting architecturally. It is a popular destination for visitors to the country.

Other important Guatamalan towns include Chichicastenango, where the majority of the people are Mayan Indians, and ancient Antigua, the old colonial capital, with impressive architecture dating back to the Spanish occupation. Both towns are interesting for their unique character and insight into Guatemalan history.

Clearing of the rainforest for agriculture continues in spite of the environmental dangers.

THE ENDANGERED RAINFOREST

The tropical rainforest is Guatemala's most precious resource. More than 700 types of trees form a thick canopy overhead and 100 feet (30 m) below, at ground level, some 4,000 types of flowering plants have been identified. New plant species that cannot be found anywhere else in the world are still being discovered in Guatemala.

The rainforests of Central and South America are also a valuable resource for modern medical research. Treatments for many illnesses and diseases have been developed by recent exploration of the rainforest, and it is thought that many more are yet to be found. Wild yams that grow in the forest have provided medical scientists with important medicines, and a species of frog has yielded a powerful anesthetic. A debate exists concerning the use of the rainforest in this way, with some arguing that foreign drug companies are exploiting the forests for financial gain without giving anything back to the country or its inhabitants. New laws are being considered to ensure local participation in future research activities.

A report in 1990 claimed that 40% of the country's forest cover had been lost since 1960. Meanwhile, clearing for agriculture continues to eat away at the country's forest reserves. With the help of international ecological groups, Guatemala has set up a large number of national parks, the most ambitious being the Maya Biosphere Reserve. It covers an area of over 4 million acres (1.6 million hectares) in northern Petén and was established with the intention of preserving the tropical rainforest. The reserve consists of a core area, where no one lives, surrounded by small farms whose inhabitants are engaged in sustainable agriculture.

In practice, however, there is a problem reconciling land conservation with the need to accommodate a growing number of Guatemalans who are moving to Petén hoping to start a new life. This includes refugees who have returned to Guatemala since the end of the civil war, which lasted 36 years. Areas within the reserve are being allocated to refugees, a move that contributes to the rapid spread of slash-and-burn farming and the further depletion of the rainforest. Posing another serious problem is illegal logging, often organized in Mexico.

EXTINCTION THROUGH TOURISM

In the late 1950s the black bass was introduced into Lake Atitlán in an attempt to create the foundations of a sport fishing industry. The black bass is a voracious feeder and one of its victims was the Atitlán grebe, a small water bird whose inability to fly made it particularly vulnerable to predators. By the mid-1960s less than a hundred survived and the numbers continued to fall as further tourist development disturbed their natural habitat. The Atitlán grebe was found nowhere else in the world; it has now been recorded as extinct.

A jaguar in the Guate-
malan rainforest.

WILDLIFE

Guatemala has a greater diversity of wildlife than any other country in Central America. More jaguars—the biggest of all cat species found in the Americas—lurk in the Petén rainforest than anywhere else in Central America. These endangered animals were revered by the ancient Maya who saw them as natural symbols of power and stealth. They carved images of the jaguar in stone and worshiped them as gods.

Like the jaguar, the puma—also known as the cougar or panther—is a forest cat that is rarely seen. It is a solitary animal that can grow to over 9 feet (3 m) in length, of which one third is the tail.

Perhaps the best known reptile found in Guatemala is the boa constrictor. This snake is not poisonous, but as its name suggests, relies on constriction to squeeze the life out of its prey before swallowing the animal whole. There are 15 species of poisonous snakes in Guatemala; one of the most common is the small but very deadly fer-de-lance. Villagers fear these far more than the huge boa constrictor because the fer-de-lance's favorite food, the common mouse, draws the snake close to the villages.

Birdlife is extraordinarily colorful and fascinating, especially in the rainforest where a

A scarlet macaw, one of the many types of parrot found in Guatemala.

variety of parrots make themselves heard as well as seen. Hummingbirds only a few inches in length share the same habitat as quetzals, which can exceed four feet (1.2 m) in length. The quetzal is Guatemala's national bird, and a reserve has been set aside near Cobán in an effort to protect it from poachers and loss of habitat. An unusual bird is the oropendola, which weaves a long nest that hangs conspicuously from trees and even telephone lines.

Guatemala's short Caribbean coast is home to the manatee, a slow-moving, aquatic mammal, rather like a seal, that was once common off the coast of Florida. Their eyesight is poor, but they are said to be able to communicate by muzzle-to-muzzle contact. They live singly or in family groups, and sometimes groups come together to form herds. Unfortunately, the manatee has been overhunted for its meat and oil and is now increasingly rare.

The mangroves on the Pacific side are important wildlife habitats and attract a variety of animal and bird life including the white ibis, the great jabiru (a large stork), raccoon, and opossum. The mangroves also provide shelter and breeding grounds for fish and crustaceans, as well as feeding and nesting areas for wading birds.

HISTORY

HUMAN HABITATION IN THE AMERICAS began around 60,000 years ago when the first humans reached North America from Asia across the Bering Strait. These early hunter-gatherers gradually worked their way south into Central America, and when the climate began to warm between 11,000 and 6,000 B.C. the stage was set for the beginning of agriculture.

There is evidence that Guatemala was inhabited around 9,000 B.C., and by about 5,000 B.C. grasses that were the ancestors of corn were known to cave dwellers in Central America. By 2,500 B.C. pre-Maya people were settled in what is now Guatemala, and some 500 years later the first farming settlements were established around lakes and rivers.

Little is known about the earliest inhabitants of Guatemala and this has encouraged various unproven, and often outlandish, theories involving early settlers from Egypt, Phoenicia, Cambodia, the "lost" kingdom of Atlantis, and even visitors from outer space.

Above: **A Mayan funeral urn in the shape of a face mask. It dates back to the eighth century A.D.**

Opposite: **The Spanish influence on Guatemalan culture is evident in the architecture of the old cities.**

PRE-CLASSIC MAYA

By 1,500 B.C. settled communities had developed and archeological discoveries suggest that the people worshiped fertility figures. They grew corn and vegetables, slept in hammocks, and began using cocoa beans as money. Between 800 and 500 B.C. the number of settlements increased substantially. It is likely that early Mayan culture in the highlands received some impetus—writing, calendar-making, and art forms—from the Olmec and Izapan civilizations in what is now Mexico.

The earliest homes were rectangular, built of mud, and protected from heavy rainfall by being set on earthen platforms raised above the ground. This was a basic design that would later be followed in the building of the great Mayan pyramid temples.

In the lowlands an important influence was the non-Maya Chicanel culture whose interest in architecture was to be passionately developed by the Maya. Just how the various influences came to bear on Mayan culture will probably never be known. But by around A.D. 300, at the time the Roman empire was entering its terminal decline, the Mayan civilization blossomed in a way that continues to fascinate and astonish historians. Some archeologists refer to this renaissance as the Maya Fluorescence.

THE MAYAN GOLDEN AGE

Mayan civilization reached its height between A.D. 300 and 900, and some idea of its amazing cultural richness can be seen in the evidence of its architecture, art, mathematics, astronomy, and writing that has managed to survive. Tikal in Petén seems to have been the cultural capital of the Mayan world, but another major site is El Mirador, in the far north of Guatemala, which is home to the largest pyramids the Maya ever built. Some of what is known about Mayan culture comes from the accounts of Spanish missionaries, who took a scholarly interest in the beliefs and practices they were intent on eliminating.

Mayan thought was at its most advanced in the field of astronomy, and considerable effort was devoted to plotting the movements of the sun, moon, and especially Venus. The Maya could predict eclipses and may have studied other planets in our solar system. Considering the fact that their calculations were made without any of the technology available to modern astronomers, the Maya were incredibly accurate. Only seven minutes separate their lunar cycle from ours, and they plotted the course of Venus with a margin of error that amounts to just two hours in five hundred years. Their mathematics included the notion of zero, a concept that did not reach Europe from the East until the Middle Ages.

The ancient Maya were a militaristic people whose young males were separated from their families and brought up as a group well-versed in the art of war. There were constant raids into neighboring communities, and prisoners were used as slaves or were ritually killed. There is evidence to suggest that different cities formed alliances through marriage.

Excavations have shown Tikal to be the most advanced Mayan city by the 6th century. Tikal covered an area of six square miles (15.5 square km), with a population estimated to be between 10,000 and 40,000. Some 3,000 buildings, ranging from temples to common huts, have been identified. Other Mayan "cities" would have been smaller but similar in concept: dispersed clusters of peasant homes with a temple serving as the center of communal activity.

Temples were vividly painted inside and out, as a few fragments still bearing original pigments can testify, and they served as a focal point for a sophisticated culture that in many ways was far more advanced than any European city around this time.

The Maya built cities around towering pyramids which served as temples to their many gods.

The history of Mayan civilization has been divided into three main periods: the Pre-Classic (2,000 B.C.–250 A.D.), the Classic (250–900 A.D.), and the Post-Classic (900–1530 A.D.).

UNEXPLAINED MYSTERY

The year A.D. 889 was a significant date in the Mayan calendar, a year that would normally have been marked in numerous stone inscriptions. Nevertheless, only three commemorative stelae (inscribed stone pillars) have been found, and historians use this as part of the evidence to suggest a collapse of the Mayan civilization beginning in A.D. 800 and lasting for a hundred years. No recorded dates have ever been found after the beginning of the 10th century, when the great temples and palaces were deserted and left to the ravages of jungle vegetation.

No acceptable explanation has been found for this dramatic demise, but hypotheses have been suggested. These include earthquakes, an invasion from Mexico, a social uprising, agricultural disaster, and rampant disease. The truth may never be known. Perhaps a number of factors combined to bring this major civilization to an end. By the time the Spanish arrived, the great Mayan cities had been deserted for 500 years.

THE SPANISH CONQUEST

The arrival of the Spanish in the early 16th century proved to be a momentous event in Guatemalan history. The terms pre-Conquest or pre-Columbian are often used as a short way of referring to Guatemalan history and culture before the Spanish conquistadors arrived.

In 1523, three years after the conquest of the Aztecs in Mexico, Hernán Cortés sent an army of some 400 Spanish and 200 Mexican soldiers south into Guatemala under the command of Pedro de Alvarado. An army of 30,000 Indians was unable to defeat the Spanish, who had the advantage of superior military technology: swords, crossbows, metal armor, gunpowder, and an early type of portable gun known as a harquebus that was supported on a tripod for ease of firing.

The Spanish also unwittingly brought another weapon in the form of European diseases, against which the Maya had no means of protection. In some areas well over half of the original population was lost to smallpox, influenza, and measles.

Eldorado, from the Spanish word for gold, was an imagined land of riches that drew the conquistadors to the Americas. They never found their dream in Guatemala, but settled down instead to the business of shipping cotton, tobacco, and chocolate back to Spain. The Spanish established their capital at Antigua, the first planned city in the Americas, but an earthquake destroyed the city in 1773.

Over two centuries of colonial rule has left its mark on Guatemalan society. Antigua and Guatemala City were founded by the Spanish. The Catholic religion, Spanish language, and a pro-Spanish social hierarchy remain today as legacies of the Spanish presence. The Indian culture, however, was not eradicated. It survived, to a large extent, by absorbing aspects of Spanish culture without sacrificing the older, Mayan beliefs.

The Church presided over the destruction of native idols and set about converting the Indian population to Catholicism.

A Franciscan or Grey Friar.   A Grey Friar or Cordelier without his Mantle.

THE POWER OF THE CHURCH

The first religious order to reach Guatemala in the wake of Alvarado's conquest was the Franciscan Order, followed by the Dominicans and then the Jesuits. The orders were granted large tracts of Indian land and soon became wealthy and powerful. In 1572 an office of the Inquisition was established in the capital with the task of identifying and punishing those who declined to convert to Christianity. By the mid-18th century the power of the Church was beginning to rival that of the Spanish government, and in 1767 the Jesuits were banned from Guatemala and other Spanish colonies.

In the early history of Spanish rule, the priests could sometimes achieve what the army found impossible. In the Verapaces, an area to the north of Guatemala City, the indigenous Achi Indians resisted the Spanish so stubbornly that Alvarado's forces gave up the attempt. A group of Dominican priests were left to pacify the Indians without the use of force.

A STRUGGLE FOR POWER

Foreign rule over Guatemala came to a quiet end in 1821 when Spain, suffering from domestic economic and political problems, relinquished all its interests in the New World. In 1823 Guatemala joined the new United Provinces of Central America. It was the only time that all of Central America was united as one nation and the capital of this confederation was Guatemala City. For Indians, though, little changed because their Spanish rulers were simply replaced by a *ladino* ("lah-DEE-no"), or Spanish-American, elite. Indians were not granted citizenship in the new United Provinces of Central America, and so the social and political imbalance remained.

A conflict emerged in the new confederation between left-wing and right-wing interests and, under the leadership of Rafael Carrera, Guatemala

Democracy is taking hold in Guatemala and elections are now generally regarded as free and fair.

SPIRITUAL SOCIALISM

Juan José Arévalo described his politics as "spiritual socialism" and he introduced sweeping economic and political reforms that gave land and ensured human rights to Indians. At every turn he was beset by attempted military coups. He was followed by another reformer, Colonel Jacobo Arbenz Guzmán, who took office as Arévalo's elected successor. Arbenz challenged the economic monopoly held by the United Fruit Company. Arbenz's government turned over two billion acres of land to small farmers, and this included unused land owned by the United Fruit Company.

In 1954, the United States government, citing communist influences within the Arbenz government, intervened with a military invasion of Guatemala that was planned by the CIA and codenamed Operation Success. It was only in May 1997, however, that the CIA openly released once-classified records disclosing how the CIA considered assassinating Arbenz. It was feared that Guatemala would have become an ally of what was then the Soviet Union unless something was done to stop the chain of events. The assassination did not take place. Arbenz fled to Cuba and then into exile in Mexico. Power passed to the army.

was declared an independent and sovereign state in 1847. In 1872 a charismatic military leader, Rufino Barrios, became president of Guatemala and initiated liberal reforms that angered the conservative Church. Unused land belonging to the Church was confiscated and sold to German immigrants to grow coffee. Barrios was excommunicated by the Pope; he responded by exiling the Archbishop of Guatemala and effectively closing down the churches. Before his assassination in 1885, Barrios had turned into a tyrant. He confiscated Maya lands and forced Indians into a system of compulsory labor on coffee plantations.

The next 60 years witnessed a struggle for power that involved countless military coups, dictators, and the growing power of the U.S. owned United Fruit Company. Only two leaders in the following 60 years managed to remain in office for any length of time and both of these were thought to be unstable in character. In 1944, popular discontent forced out Jorge Ubico, a tyrant who ruled for 14 years and believed himself to be a reincarnation of Napoleon. In the following year the most democratic elections in the country's history took place, and Juan José Arévalo became president with 85% of the vote. The new mood of reform was so popular that the change of power was dubbed "The 1944 Revolution."

MILITARY RULE AND CIVIL WAR

Political divisions between the right-wing faction, which supported the traditional ruling interests, and the left-wing faction, which fought for social reform, split Guatemala. Governments that supported the United Fruit Company were opposed by growing bands of peasants who formed a guerrilla opposition.

The civil war started in 1960 and the military began a campaign of terrorism and slaughter. During the four years of Colonel Arana Osorio's presidency that began in 1970, an estimated 15,000 people were killed by military death squads. General elections continued to take place, but mostly it was the military leaders who assumed political power. An estimated 25,000 Guatemalans were killed during the García presidency that began in 1978.

PEACE AT LAST

The government elected in 1990 offered to investigate the abuse of human rights, but corruption persisted and dissidents continued to "disappear." A group of Norwegian mediators started a peace process that eventually led to the end of the civil war. Public demonstrations helped to establish a new government in 1994 that continued to hold out the prospect of peace. The following year, 1995, was declared "El Año de la Maya" (The Year of the Maya), and the military and the guerrillas began to discuss a lasting peace.

New elections were held in 1996 but over 60% of the electorate did not bother to vote. The new government under Alvaro Arzú pursued peace talks, and in December 1996, an agreement on a permanent ceasefire was signed by the adversaries in Latin America's longest civil war. A conflict that had lasted 36 years finally ended after claiming at least 100,000 lives.

At one stage, under President Carter, the United States withdrew its military and financial support for the Guatemalan government. The Reagan administration, however, restored military aid.

GOVERNMENT

A NEW ERA IN THE GOVERNMENT of Guatemala began with the 1996 election of Alvaro Arzú as president. His party, the National Advancement Party (PAN), won 51% of the vote by narrowly defeating another right-wing party, the Guatemalan Republican Front (FRG). In one sense it was not a great victory for democracy because 63% of the electorate abstained from voting. In another sense, though, the election was significant because Arzú committed his government to making peace with the Guatemalan National Revolutionary Unit (URNG), the armed guerrilla opposition.

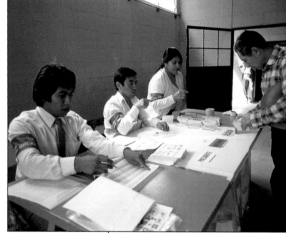

Above: **A Guatemalan voting station.**

Opposite: **The national flag is flown in front of government offices.**

Under the terms of the peace accord the army is required to relinquish its role in domestic security and leave this to a new police force. The traditional role of an army in a democracy is non-political, defending the country from external threats, and it is hoped that under the new agreement Guatemala will no longer live with the threat of military commanders seizing control of the country. Various paramilitary groups that were involved in the systematic abuse of human rights will be abolished. In the immediate wake of the peace accord, the government announced the closure of five military bases, and early in 1997 the United Nations approved the deployment of a military mission to supervise the disarmament and demobilization of some 3,000 URNG soldiers.

THE CONSTITUTION

The constitution, which was drawn up in 1986, remains the basis for government in Guatemala. The country is defined constitutionally as a democratic republic and power is divided among a legislature, an executive position of power, and a judiciary.

The legislature, which makes the laws, is called the National Congress, and is elected every five years by universal suffrage. Out of the total of 80 seats, 16 are elected through a nationwide ballot and the other 64 are elected in departmental districts. The National Congress is a unicameral legislature, meaning there is just one chamber, not two as in the United States.

Executive power rests with the president, who is directly elected by universal suffrage, and the vice-president. Individuals standing for the presidency, vice-presidency, or a seat in Congress must belong to and be nominated by authorized political parties. The main restriction on the authorization of political parties is that they must not be committed to the overthrow of the democratic process. The judiciary, concerned with courts of law and the interpretation of laws, is ruled by the Supreme Court of Justice. Under the power of the Supreme Court are nine justices, each elected to their positions for four years by Congress.

For the purposes of administration, the country is divided into a number of *departamentos* ("di-par-tuh-MEN-tos"), each of which has its own governor. Petén, for example, is a department divided into a number of municipalities that operate through elected councils and mayors. Independent candidates, not affiliated to a political party, are allowed to stand for election at this level.

SHARING LOCAL GOVERNMENT

In predominantly Indian regions of the country, local government often takes two forms: one for the Indian population and one for the ladinos. In the major town of Chichicastenango, for example, there are two sets of local officials. The central government appoints officers, but Indians elect their own civil officials. The local government that is elected by Indians has its own mayor and its own local court for dealing with offenses committed by local Indians.

THE PRESIDENT

The president of Guatemala is elected for a single, five-year term and during that time the president is the head of state and head of government. A president does not always need the support of a majority of the population in order to get elected. For example, universal suffrage was abolished by the military in the 1950s, and in the 1970 election, when only half the electorate voted, Colonel Osorio polled just under half the votes. This amounted to around 4% of the population voting for the new president. This pattern was repeated in the 1996 elections.

Although the army has no political role according to the constitution, it has played a significant part in the recent history of Guatemalan politics. Between 1954—when a democratically elected government was overthrown—and the 1990s, a number of Guatemala's presidents have been army officers.

The presidential palace in Guatemala City.

31

THE FIRST GOVERNOR OF GUATEMALA

Pedro de Alvarado was a deputy to Cortés, the Spanish conqueror of Mexico, and was 39 years old when he was sent south to claim Indian territory for the Spanish Crown, establish and promote the Catholic faith among the pagan natives, and collect as much gold as possible. Mayan history records a legendary personal duel between Alvarado and an Indian king, Tecún Umánd, in which the Spaniard emerged the victor. Alvarado was also unwittingly aided by European diseases like measles and smallpox, because the Indians had no natural resistance to these diseases. It took Alvarado over six years to establish control over the country, but within three years of arriving he established a capital close to Antigua and had his own palace built using captured Indians as slave labor. His reputation for cruelty got him recalled to Spain at one stage, but he later returned to Guatemala. He ruled Guatemala as his personal kingdom and grew exceedingly rich, but his restless nature drove him first to Peru and then to Mexico in 1541 where he died.

His wife, Beatrz de la Cueva, is said to have ordered the palace in Antigua to be painted black both inside and out on hearing of her husband's death. She also proclaimed herself governess, but, within the space of one day an earthquake led to a mud slide that buried the whole city. Beatrz de la Cueva was governess for 24 hours. She was the first, and as yet the last, woman to rule Guatemala.

THE ARMY

The army has played an infamous role in Guatemalan government. After the military coup in 1954, power passed to the head of the country's army, and over the next 30 years the country became violently divided socially and politically. Conservative groups, especially business groups and the large landowners who distrusted democracy because they thought it would weaken their economic power, turned to the military to suppress political

opposition. The army pursued this agenda ruthlessly and with a disregard for human rights that shocked most of the world. Colonel Osorio, who ruled from 1970 to 1974, declared: "If it is necessary to turn the country into a cemetery in order to pacify it, I will not hesitate to do so."

Under the 1996 peace accord, the size of the army will be reduced by one-third from its present force of 46,000. It will also lose one-third of its budget. What remains uncertain is whether the army officers who committed violent crimes against civilians will be brought to justice.

In line with this new curb on the army's political power, the role of the police force has also been redefined. Whereas the police may have once been considered an instrument of the ruling party, they are now more concerned with the justice system rather than politics. Guatemala has been helped in its move toward democracy by the relative stability now evident in the region. It is hoped by many that new economic opportunities will improve the lives of Guatemalans, and lead to new roles for the army and the police in protection and defense rather than oppression.

An army training camp. The role of the army has changed since the peace accord ending the civil war came into effect.

THE OPPOSITION

The groups that until 1996 operated as armed guerrillas represent various alternative voices in the government of Guatemala. For over 35 years such groups, supported mainly by the Indians, have been excluded from mainstream politics. Early guerrilla groups were called the Guerrilla Army of the Poor and the Organization of the People in Arms, but over time the Guatemalan National Revolutionary Unit (URNG) emerged as the main opposition to the government.

The political fracturing of Guatemalan society began in 1960 when two army officers, who were against the level of corruption and incompetence in the government, fled to the eastern highlands. They were soon joined by other groups who also felt alienated. By the end of the 1960s the first wave of armed opposition had been virtually defeated, but the continuation of military rule through the 1970s fostered ongoing armed opposition. Demands for human rights and social justice fell on deaf ears, and

A MILITARY DICTATOR

General Enrique Peralta Azurdia (1909–97) was a military dictator in the 1960s, and although he is largely forgotten by most Guatemalans today, his career typifies the role of the military in Guatemalan government.

Elections were due in 1964. On March 29, 1963, José Arévalo returned to Guatemala. Arévalo was famous as the liberal reformer whose rule as civilian president in the 1950s launched a genuine attempt to modernize the country. His arrival scared the conservative groups in power, who feared that Arévalo might win the election, and Peralta was at the head of a successful coup that took place on March 30. Peralta organized his own death squads and other political parties found it dangerous to oppose him. Organizers of trade unions "disappeared," and when elections finally took place in 1966, the main civilian candidate was assassinated.

members of legitimate political parties who did not support the military were murdered. In the cities a large number of politicians, academics, priests, trade unionists, teachers, and lawyers were killed. In the countryside an even larger number of Indian peasants were killed. Between 1978 and 1982 an estimated 25,000 were killed by the army. The brutal suppression of political opponents became so blatant that the United States, under President Carter, suspended military aid to the Guatemalan government in 1977. It was restored in 1982.

The imprisonment and murder of political opponents continued throughout the 1980s and well into the 1990s. Under the terms of the peace accord, the URNG was required to hand over all its weapons, and its 3,000 members disbanded. In time, at least one new political party will announce itself as the peacetime heir to the URNG. Early in 1997 the United Nations sent military observers to Guatemala to oversee the disarmament and demobilization of the guerrilla army that had opposed government forces for 36 years.

Guatemala's coat of arms.

THE NATIONAL FLAG

The Guatemalan national flag has three vertical bands of light blue, white, and light blue. The white band includes the coat of arms, which is composed of a green and red quetzal and a scroll superimposed on a pair of crossed rifles and crossed swords, framed by a wreath. The scroll bears the inscription *Libertad 15 de Settembre de 1821*, referring to the original date of independence from Spain.

ECONOMY

GUATEMALA'S MARKET ECONOMY is based primarily on agriculture, with over half the workforce employed on the farms, ranches, and plantations that account for one-quarter of the gross national product and three-fifths of all exports. About one-quarter of the workforce is employed in service and manufacturing industries such as food processing, pharmaceuticals, rubber, paper, and textiles. Some 7% work in commerce, 4% in construction work, and 3% in transport.

The country's most productive soil is found in the highlands and along the coastal plain, and it is in these areas, not surprisingly, that most of the economically important farms and plantations are situated. Big farms that grow corn are in the highlands, while the coastal plain is devoted mostly to coffee, sugarcane, and fruit. There are very large cattle ranches closer to the Pacific coast. In the highlands most farms are small, traditional ones where corn, beans, and squash are cultivated, mainly for domestic consumption.

Guatemala City is the focus of nearly all industrial and commercial businesses; one disadvantage of this is that the capital suffers from pollution and congestion. Thousands of unemployed Guatemalans flock to the city in the hope of finding work. New shanty dwellings have sprung up to accommodate them.

Guatemala has become one of the world's major suppliers of cardamom, a spice in the ginger family. There is also a small fishing industry centered around the Pacific Ocean. Other small but developing industries deal in petroleum and the mining of antimony, iron ore, and lead. The oil industry is mostly based in Petén and is one of the threats to Petén's rainforests.

Above: **A Guatemalan street vendor.**

Opposite: **From agriculture to heavy industry, Guatemala is a market economy. But it is on the streets and in the daily lives of Guatemalans that the marketplace is most visible.**

After coffee, sugarcane is the nation's largest export commodity.

EXPORTS AND IMPORTS

Coffee is the single most important export, accounting for about 20% of the country's total exports. Sugar is the next largest export, accounting for over 12%, followed by bananas, cardamom, and cotton. There is also a healthy market exporting vegetables, fruit, and flowers. The main market for all these exports is the United States, but other important trading nations are Germany, El Salvador, and Japan.

The United States is also the most important trading partner in terms of imports, accounting for over 40% of all imports. Mexico and Venezuela provide essential supplies of petroleum. Japan and Germany are also trading partners. From the United States, Guatemala imports electrical machinery, metal products, and chemical products mostly used in the country's own industrial production. Textiles and food are also imported.

Santo Tomás de Castilla, situated on the Caribbean coast, is the country's main port.

INDUSTRY

In Guatemala over 15% of the gross national product is accounted for by industrial activity. Most of the small factories and industrial concerns are based in and around Guatemala City.

The main industrial activities are concerned with the processing of food, tobacco, and sugar. There are also small industries involved in the manufacturing of textiles and clothes, tires, cement, and pharmaceuticals. Most of these products find their primary markets in the United States. Some petroleum refining also takes place. Although it currently accounts for less than 5% of the gross national product, it is an industry that has potential for development.

The service sector is the largest contributor to the economy and employs 38% of the workforce. This is expected to grow even further as more tourists are attracted to Guatemala by its archeological and geographical sights. Official unemployment figures are quite low and stood at around 4.8% in 1994.

Timber is a valuable export resource but is at odds with efforts to preserve the rainforests.

CARDAMOM

Cardamom is a spice that comes from *Elettaria cardamomum*, a member of the ginger family. In Guatemala the plants grow up to a height of 20 feet (6 m) and produce long, flowering shoots. The petals are greenish with a purplish white lip. The fruit is dried in the sun after picking, turning from a bright red to a dark brown color.

Cardamom seeds have an aromatic flavor and are popularly used as seasoning in curries. Spicy dishes in the United States often contain cardamom that is likely to have come from Guatemala, the world's largest exporter of cardamom. Exports of Guatemalan cardamom go mostly to the Arabian Gulf states because of the popularity of cardamom-flavored coffee in countries like Saudi Arabia.

In the Alta Verapaz region of the highlands, about 62 miles (100 km) north of the capital, the cultivation of cardamom is vital to the local economy, as up to 200,000 people earn their living from the spice. The Alta Verapaz region was where the first cardamom seeds were planted; they were brought there from India by Germans who, at the time, were heavily involved in the coffee industry.

COFFEE—SMOKY AND SPICY

Guatemala produces more coffee than any other country in Central America. As an industry it is prone to price fluctuations and is dependent on favorable weather conditions, but in recent years the market price of coffee beans has remained relatively stable. Guatemalan coffee is noted for the smoky, spicy flavor that makes it one of the world's best.

The story of Guatemalan coffee goes back to the early years of Spanish rule when the Jesuits cultivated coffee trees as ornamental plants. In the second half of the 19th century a rise in world demand led to the rapid

expansion of coffee plantations, mostly run by German immigrants. Indians were forced off their land to make way for plantations and were subsequently made to work on the plantations. By 1914 German immigrants owned half the land that was being used for coffee production, and as much as 50% of the country's total yield of coffee was being exported to Germany. Most of the Germans were expelled from Guatemala during World War II, but the coffee industrialists remain a powerful economic and political force.

Coffee farming in Guatemala posed a few problems to the early growers but German immigrants evolved a process that involved protecting coffee trees during periods of cold weather. Pitch was burned close to the plantations; the dense smoke kept the frost away from the trees and also imparted a smoky flavor to the coffee. The rich volcanic soil and an ideal temperature made it possible for a variety of coffee beans to be cultivated in the country, with the highest quality beans growing at an altitude of around 5,000 feet (1,520 m).

Coffee beans before the harvest. Coffee is Guatemala's most important export product.

A BANANA REPUBLIC

Some 30 miles (50 km) inland from the Caribbean coast, to the east of Lake Izabal, lies the small town of Bananera. As the name suggests, this is banana territory, producing the bulk of the two billion bananas exported from Guatemala each year. The origin of the town's name goes back to the 19th century when the United Fruit Company, a U.S. company, chose the town as the headquarters of its banana-exporting business. At the time there was no suitable transport infrastructure and the company built its own railways and developed the port of Puerto Barrios. The demand for bananas in the United States appeared insatiable, growing at a phenomenal rate in the last three decades of the 19th century. As 1900 approached, over 16 million bananas per year were being consumed in the United States, and they all came from Guatemala through the United Fruit Company.

Once a mainstay of the economy, bananas are now part of a more diverse agricultural export industry.

In some respects the United Fruit Company was very enlightened, providing health care and housing for its employees. It also made massive profits because wages were low and company taxes were almost nonexistent. In time, the company's tremendous power grew to such an extent that virtually the entire Guatemalan economy was in its hands and depended on the company's support. Proof of its power came in 1954 when attempts to take over unused company land by a reform government led directly to the installment of a new, unelected government that supported the company.

The United Fruit Company no longer exists and its interests in Guatemala are now part of the Del Monte corporation. Exporting bananas is still very important to the country's economy and large banana plantations still surround the town of Bananera.

TOURISM

In recent years the annual amount of money spent by tourists in Guatemala has averaged US$250 million, and this covers years when many potential visitors were discouraged by outbreaks of violence and evidence of the systematic abuse of human rights. The new era of peace is likely to usher in a period of growth and development that will make tourism a significant contributor to the country's economy.

It is also possible that revenue gained through tourism will reach a wider section of the population than the small elite that currently enjoys a disproportionate amount of the country's wealth earned through export industries. Tourists visiting Guatemala are often more likely to spend their money among the people who operate market stalls or guided tours. This in turn means that the money is redistributed within the lower levels of the domestic economy.

The United Fruit Company acquired the nickname El Pulpo ("ell PULL-poh"), Spanish for octopus, because of the way it managed to exert influence over so many different parts of the country's economy.

Tourism is set to become one of the country's major industries. Visitors are attracted to Guatemala for its scenic beauty and diverse ecosystems.

Many of the more popular destinations for visitors are in the Petén area, especially Tikal, and enterprising Indian families able to offer accommodation or sell locally-produced handicrafts are the ones most likely to benefit from tourism.

The highlands, too, attract many visitors because of the cultural integrity of the Indian society, the splendid Mayan ruins, and the exciting spectacle of the world's largest Indian market in Chichicastenango. Antigua, the original capital, is popular because of its 18th century colonial architecture and relaxed atmosphere. Lake Atitlán is one of the scenic areas in the country and a prime tourist attraction.

Over the next few decades, as the tourist industry grows in Guatemala, there is a danger that the physical and cultural environment will suffer as a consequence. Ecotourism offers the best hope of allowing Guatemalans to benefit from tourists without affecting the quality of their culture in the process.

ECOTOURISM

Ecotourism is based on the idea that it is possible to encourage and benefit from tourism without inflicting irreversible damage on the host culture. This concept involves educating both visitors and local people. The success of this approach in neighboring Belize and Costa Rica has shown that the program is a realistic one. The rainforest in Petén, for example, has tremendous short-term, economic value as a source of timber, but as the largest surviving tract of tropical rainforest in North America, it offers the long-term promise of being more valuable as an ecotourist destination. Local people, with their knowledge of flora and fauna, can find employment as guides, and many visitors who are attracted to ecological vacations are more than content to skip luxury hotels in favor of humble but authentic accommodation provided by the local population. Both the making and wearing of traditional Indian dress has increased over recent years; this has been partly attributed to the growing realization that there is a commercial market for cultural handicrafts.

Tourism is the fastest growing sector of Guatemala's economy, having grown by more than 500% over the last 10 years. It is hoped that ecotourism will become the characteristic form of this rapidly developing industry and economic resource. A healthy start to ecotourism has begun with the success of the Tikal National Park, a protected area that covers 222 square miles (575 square km) and includes ancient Mayan ruins.

GUATEMALANS

THERE ARE OVER TEN MILLION PEOPLE living in Guatemala, mostly either Indians or ladinos. Indians constitute more than half of the population, making Guatemala the only country in the world where American Indians are a majority. Portraits of ancient Maya people inscribed in stone have the same facial characteristics as contemporary Indians. When the Spanish arrived in 1523, the whole country was populated by Indians, but the impact of European diseases on the indigenous population was devastating. In some regions over 75% of the population died; it was not until the end of the 17th century that the Indian population regained its pre-Columbian level. By that time a significant amount of intermarriage between those of Spanish heritage and the Indian population had produced a new people, known as ladinos.

Above: **Indian sisters wearing the colorful, traditional dress characteristic of native Guatemalans.**

Opposite: **Young Ladino woman from Guatemala City.**

Today ladinos account for over 40% of the population. They wear Western-style clothing, generally enjoy a higher standard of living than the Indians, and tend to dominate positions of power and influence in the country. Nearly all the larger commercial establishments are owned by ladinos, as are all the large tracts of privately-owned land. The 1996 peace accord provides an opportunity to redress the social and political inequality between the Indians and ladinos. In 1997 Rigoberta Menchú, the award-winning Indian writer, was offered a ministerial post in the government as part of this process.

As a whole, 43% of the population are under 15 years of age, 4% are senior citizens over the age of 65, and the remainder, aged between 15 and 64, make up just over half the population. The population is growing at the rate of 2.5% annually.

INDIANS

Maya Indians are spread across Central America. Some 20% of them live in southern Mexico, Honduras, and Belize, while the other 80% are concentrated in Guatemala. Seven out of every eight Indians in the Americas live in Guatemala. Around 1900 about 80% of the country's population was Maya, but this percentage has now dropped to just over half.

There are different groups within Central America's Indian population. The Mam people inhabit the northwest highlands, the Quiché are concentrated in the midwestern highlands, and the eastern highlands are home to the Pokomam. These are the largest groupings and each of these is divided into smaller groups with their own language. The Quiché group includes the Cakchiquel, and the Pokomam includes the Kekchí.

Most of the Indians of modern Guatemala share certain physical characteristics. They tend to be short but stocky, with straight, black hair, dark eyes, and a skin color that ranges from copper to brown. The face is relatively broad, with high cheekbones and a low forehead.

INDIAN FEMALE DRESS

The exotic colors of traditional Indian dress, which helped Guatemala win the Miss Universe native costume competition in 1967, make the workaday clothes of Americans or Europeans seem quite dull and unimaginative by comparison. Women's dress has managed to retain more continuity with the Mayan past than male attire.

Pride of place goes to the *huipil* ("WEE-pil"), a roomy, sleeveless tunic or overblouse that was once worn loose but which is now tucked into a wraparound or gathered skirt. Women often add a touch of individuality to their skirts by sewing in colored strips of embroidered cloth, known as

Guatemala's Indians are the direct descendants of the Maya people who plotted the course of Venus and built pyramid temples over a thousand years ago.

randa ("RAND-ah"). There is also a traditional cape, worn around the shoulders, and various waist sashes. Blouses are commonly worn, although these are a legacy of Spanish culture.

What clearly distinguishes all these items of dress is not so much the basic design but rather their sophisticated and colorful embroidery. Pictorial themes based on indigenous as well as mythical and magical flora and fauna are very popular, and it is believed that many of the patterns have a direct lineage from ancient Mayan culture. In recent years, following the success of literacy campaigns, *huipils* have been embroidered with the name of the wearer's village. The more intricately decorated *huipils* take months to make, especially when a complicated pattern is woven into the fabric using a backstrap loom. Women sometimes wear their best *huipils* inside out, so as to lengthen the life of the embroidery, and only wear their garment for a special outing like market day or a fiesta.

Different village communities have their own traditional embroidery patterns, and a woman's home village can be identified from her dress. In the village of Santiago Atitlán near Lake Atitlán, for example, the women's *huipils* are colored with white and purple stripes. They also wear the *tocayal* ("toe-CAY-al"), a bright red headwrap, which is depicted on one of the country's coins.

The town of Nahualá has a characteristic symbol of a twin-headed eagle, thought to be part of the symbolic regalia of the Hapsburg family that ruled Spain at the time when Guatemala was colonized.

Traditional embroidery patterns identify the area the wearer comes from. For Indians, traditional dress is an important link to their culture and heritage.

Outside of the larger cities some Indian men still dress in the traditional style.

INDIAN MALE DRESS

Indian male dress shows more evidence of Spanish influence, but there are traditional touches that men add to their attire. This is very evident in the area around the town of Sololá in the highlands, where the Indians are famous for their traditional clothes. When the British writer Aldous Huxley visited the market in the 1930s he described it as "a walking museum of fancy dress."

Traditional Indian men's dress includes short baggy trousers that are embroidered like their jackets and complemented by colorful cowboy shirts. Their jackets are often relatively plain, in simple black and white with frogging, but on the back there is often an emblematic bat. The bat was the symbol of the Mayan royal family who were the rulers before the Spanish arrived.

The *ponchito* ("pon-CHEE-toe") is a woolen blanket, usually made on a foot-loom, that many men wear over their trousers. *Ponchito* is the name given to the shorter version, while the longer version is called a *rodillera* ("row-dee-YEH-rah"). There are some interesting regional differences in the way this is worn. In Sololá it is worn around the hips with a belt, and a folded section at the top covers the belt. In other areas the *ponchito* is a lot smaller and is only worn in front like an apron. Sometimes the *ponchito* is embroidered with a colorful band at each end and has a white border.

Hats are commonly worn by men, and they come in a variety of sizes. They are made from straw, wool, or even palm leaf. More expensive leather hats are worn for special occasions.

Many men, even if they are attired in Western trousers and a dress shirt, carry a small traditional shoulder bag made from wool.

THE PLIGHT OF INDIANS

The unfortunate plight of Guatemalan Indians began in the early years of the Spanish conquest when the conquistadors were given land rights as a reward for their services. In addition to land, the Spanish were entitled to demand native labor without pay, and they could also tax them through enforced contributions of goods such as cloth and salt.

There were five Indian revolts in the 18th century and seven in the 19th century—all were brutally suppressed. Long after the abolition of slavery, the Maya continued to be treated as slaves, and even well into the 19th century it was not uncommon to find peasants who were forced to work for their landowners as a means of repaying a "loan." In reality the loan could never be repaid, and the peasant remained a virtual slave.

In the 1930s laws were passed obliging Indians to work on plantations. It was not until the socialist governments of 1945 to 1954 that the plight of the Indians was seriously acknowledged. In spite of this Indians continued to suffer.

After the United States sponsored military coup in 1954, and under the military governments that followed, the Indians were treated in much the same way as they were under the Spanish. The chief victims of the systematic abuse of human rights by the military in recent decades have also been the indigenous Indians because it was to the Indians that various guerrilla movements turned for support. It is hoped by many that the new peace accord will lead to significant improvements for Indians and their culture.

There are about 150 villages in Guatemala where the local Indian women wear traditional dress with designs and colored patterns unique to that particular village. In only about 20 villages can the same be said of Indian men.

HEADDRESSES AND SANDALS

The stone carvings of the ancient Maya include interesting details of dress. Although contemporary Guatemalans no longer deck themselves out in headdresses made of quetzal feathers as the Maya did, Indian women do like elaborate and visually arresting headdresses.

The female villagers of Santiago Atitlán are particularly renowned for their headdresses, which are made from strips of colored cloth over 30 feet (9 m) in length. The cloth is continuously coiled around the head to form an impressive halo. The women of Aguacatán, also in the western highlands, are equally famous for their turbans made from multicolored pieces of cloth.

Another example of continuity in Indian dress may be found in the highbacked sandals clearly shown in some of the ancient stone carvings. In some parts of Guatemala today, both men and women can be seen wearing sandals that look very similar to those worn by their ancestors. The ancient Maya, however, never used the kind of sandals worn by poorer people today, made from discarded tires and tied together with thongs.

LADINOS

Ladinos, who make up about 42% of the population, are usually described as people of mixed Spanish and Indian blood. Sometimes, though, the term is not used in a racial sense but may be used to describe an Indian who has forsaken traditional Indian dress and customs and adopted the culture inherited from Spain. Across Central America the general term for people of mixed Spanish and Indian blood is *mestizo* ("mes-TEE-so"); only in Guatemala are they known as ladino. The term itself is a Spanish one and denotes one of the 16 racial castes that divided the population under Spanish colonial law.

There are no Guatemalans of pure Spanish descent and the term ladino does not carry any derogatory implications. Ladinos speak Spanish and they tend not to acknowledge their obvious kinship with Mayan Indians, some even going so far as to claim that their ancestors were not Maya but Aztec or Toltec, Indians who came to Guatemala from Mexico and intermarried with the Spanish. It is more likely that Spanish soldiers, most

Of mixed Spanish and Indian blood, these young Ladinos are the face of modern, urban Guatemala.

of whom would not have been allowed to bring wives with them from Spain, married Indian women. In some cases this would have been Mayan Indians, but because the Maya were reluctant to marry outside of their own racial group, it would also have included Indians from other parts of Central America.

Ladino culture is centered around Guatemala City for historical reasons because the capital was the seat of Spanish power, and this was where Indians interacted with the Spanish. Today most ladinos live in the towns and cities of the western highlands where they make up three-quarters of the population. They largely control the commerce and politics of their locality. While most Indians are farmers, ladinos are more likely to work in shops, government departments, or as paid laborers in industry.

MINORITY GROUPS

An interesting minority group in Guatemala called the garifuna (formerly known as Black Caribs) live around Livingston on the Caribbean coast. The town has a

Many foreigners come to Guatemala to improve their Spanish. Antigua is well known for its language schools.

population of only 3,000, but this is the only place in Guatemala where a garifuna community can be found.

The garifuna have a highly unusual history that goes back centuries to when Carib Indians and African slaves, exiled from British colonies in the Caribbean, made a home on the Caribbean island of St. Vincent. In the 17th century descendants of these people migrated to Central America. Their culture combines traditional Indian beliefs with elements of African thought, but today their African ethnicity and cultural distinctiveness is gradually being diluted to the point of extinction.

Some 3% of Guatemala's population is neither Indian nor ladino, being mostly from the United States and Europe, Germany in particular. Their economic importance to the country is far greater than this small percentage indicates, as many of them are powerful industrialists or owners of large ranches. For a long time, the U.S. based United Fruit Company accounted for a small but very powerful group of American expatriates, although the company no longer operates in Guatemala. Some of the Germans living in Guatemala can trace their families back to the late 19th century when President Barrios sold land to German farmers to grow coffee. Non-Guatemalan white people are generally referred to as "gringos," and because of the fact that most visitors to the country come from the United States, the term gringo is often used to mean a citizen of the United States.

Popular names for boys in Guatemala are Mateo, Juan, Carlos, Edwin, Roberto, and Miguel. Popular girls' names are Maria, Lucrecia, and Ana. Everyone also has a second name and a typical name might be Ana Maria or Miguel Angel.

REFUGEES

During the 1970s and early 1980s the level of persecution against the Indian population led to thousands fleeing Guatemala to seek safety in Mexico and other countries. The new climate of peace has seen about 25,000 refugees returning to their country. Another 40,000 refugees live in United Nations camps in Mexico. In addition to this there are countless thousands of Guatemalans living illegally in Mexico and the United States who are now considering returning. A new government amnesty has resulted in the emergence of large groups of refugees who had remained in hiding in the more remote corners of Guatemala. Over the next few years all of these people will be seeking reintegration into Guatemalan society and trying to begin a new life.

One of the many problems facing the refugees is where to settle. The shantytowns of Guatemala City can only offer a life of poverty, thus the underpopulated lowlands of Petén are attracting an increasing number of refugees. This causes problems of another kind as their use of slash-and-burn agriculture is depleting the rainforest.

LIFESTYLE

THERE ARE TWO BASIC LIFESTYLES in Guatemala: that of the mostly urban ladino class and that of the mostly rural Indian people. Wealth is so unevenly distributed that a Mayan family earns about half as much as a ladino family. More Indian males than females move to urban areas and coastal plantations looking for work, and perhaps not surprisingly, once they are away from their own community there is a tendency for ladino values to affect their lifestyle. Sociologists refer to this tendency as a process of "ladinization."

The ladino lifestyle is recognizably Western, not just in terms of dress but also in terms of consumer values and a generally materialistic attitude. Mayan lifestyle does not dismiss the benefits of consumer goods and appliances, but their acquisitions are usually seen in terms of gaining respect within the community, where notions of honor and honesty are still important. Indians rarely marry outside their community. The basic difference between the ladino and Indian cultures goes back to Spanish colonial rule. The Spanish regarded the Indians as ignorant pagans. The unfortunate legacy of this in modern Guatemala is that the population is still affected by racist attitudes.

Traditionally Mayan women have been important to the survival of Indian culture; even when they are exposed to ladino values, working as live-in maids or as workers in assembly line factories around Guatemala City, they still tend to steadfastly hold on to their traditional lifestyle. However, while many an Indian male may live and work in a city, speak Spanish most of the time, and wear Western dress, he still thinks of himself as an Indian and returns periodically to his home village where he speaks his Indian language and participates in local customs and festivals.

Above: **A Western lifestyle is more prominent in the cities of Guatemala.**

Opposite: **In rural parts communal laundry areas are still used. They provide an important point of social contact as well as a place to wash clothes.**

Poverty remains a problem in Guatemala. These rural dwellings have been constructed from whatever the family could find nearby. In the cities too, shantytowns are common, and the lack of hygienic conditions poses a health risk to the population.

POVERTY

Most Guatemalans are poor and not just by comparison to the United States. The average income of a Guatemalan is one-sixteenth that of an American and a third that of a Mexican. A typical Mexican will live 10 years longer than a Guatemalan, and the number of hospital beds in Guatemala, in proportion to its population, is half that of Mexico's. According to the World Bank, over 80% of the population live in poverty.

There are blatant inequalities within the country. A small minority of relatively rich people live in the suburbs of Guatemala City, enjoying modern amenities as part of an affluent lifestyle that is completely foreign, not just to the vast majority of the population but also to most of the other people living in the capital. Every week hundreds of poverty-stricken peasants arrive in Guatemala City hoping for work. Rambling shantytowns continue to spread around the outskirts of the city. The more affluent ladino residents tend to resent this so Indians find themselves disadvantaged when it comes to finding employment.

MIGRATING FOR WORK

Migration is a fact of life in Guatemala and few families, whether Indian or ladino, are unaffected by it. Sons and daughters of wealthy provincial families as well as the mass of poorer people leave their homes to find employment in urban areas. More ladinos than Indians migrate to Guatemala City, although Indian migration from the highlands to the coastal plantations is also very common. It is often conducted on a seasonal basis, with Indians returning to their villages and farms at important times like the planting and harvesting of the corn.

In the countryside much of the best land was forcibly taken in the past for coffee plantations so Indians generally have to struggle to survive. An extreme example of this struggle for survival is shown by the need of some farmers on very hilly and high ground to tie themselves by rope to a tree in order to till the ground.

HEALTH

The general level of health care in Guatemala is very poor, and there are serious health problems. The average life expectancy is about 61 years for men and 66 for women, with ladinos usually living 10 to 15 years longer than Indians. Part of the problem is not just a lack of hospitals, doctors, nurses, and health care centers, but a major imbalance in the distribution of medical facilities. Guatemala City has about three-quarters of all the country's doctors but only about 20% of the population live in the capital. The lack of proper facilities and medical personnel in the countryside helps account for the high infant mortality rate: more than one in three children die before the age of 3. Aspects of health care that are taken for granted in the United States—inoculation against measles, for example—are sadly deficient for the majority of Guatemalans. While access to running water is available to most homes in urban areas, in the countryside less than half the population have running water.

The poverty that afflicts so many people's lives results in very poor nutrition, and this is a major factor in poor health. Pregnant mothers who lack proper meals give birth to underweight babies that are especially vulnerable to infant illnesses. The main causes of infant mortality are diarrhea, respiratory infections, and childbirth problems, all of which are

More than half of the workforce are employed in agriculture, but less than 2% of landowners own over 65% of the land.

An army medical team conducts a clinic in one of Guatemala's poorer rural communities.

relatively easy to prevent with the necessary resources. Those who do survive often face a childhood characterized by a poor diet and a lack of vitamins. Indeed, malnutrition, along with infectious diseases, could be drastically reduced if an effective health care program for the rural population was put in place.

RURAL LIFE

Well over half the population live in rural areas, but the land is not fully utilized. Large landowners are not obliged to use all their land and large tracts remain unexploited. The land that is farmed by an Indian family may be hours away from their home and situated high up the side of a mountain or on the slopes of a volcano. Typical rural villages suffer from serious underdevelopment; a very obvious sign of this is the lack of a proper transportation system. Most roads that link villages in the countryside are unpaved and unmaintained so that fallen rocks and broken stones impede travel to the extent that a rider on horseback is able to travel almost as fast as the driver of a four-wheel-drive vehicle. Many villages have no connecting roads that can be used by any type of vehicle. It was not until 1970 that the first road was built linking northern Petén with the rest of the country.

Most villages now have electricity, but most families cannot afford it. Bottled gas is also too expensive for many families so firewood is collected as fuel for cooking and for keeping warm at night. Most homes have no running water or toilet facilities. Women collect water from a communal

standpipe and carry it home in containers balanced on their heads. The washing of clothes also takes place at communal washing places or on the banks of a local river.

The farming of corn is traditionally men's work. Women can inherit land and usually manage secondary crops like beans and vegetables and look after the family's livestock.

Cash crops like chilies and fruit are cultivated whenever possible and sold at the weekly village market. Also sold at the market are the chickens, turkeys, or pigs that are commonly found on an Indian farm, but are rarely killed for the table. Occasionally a chicken is cooked for a family feast at a local festival.

Children as young as 7 or 8 sometimes work alongside their parents on the family land and function productively as part of the family. The skills needed to make a living from the land are passed on from one generation to the next, but these days it is common for young adults to leave the land behind and seek work in the cities.

Father and son work the land with the help of cattle. Plowing the ash back into the ground after burning the forest to clear land adds valuable nutrients to the soil.

FARMING CORN

Most Mayan Indians are subsistence farmers and their plots of land are an important mark of their identity. The land produces beans and corn. The Mayan attitude to land is a religious one, arising from the vital economic importance of corn.

Corn seeds are planted in furrows and when they sprout the farmer protects them with a small mound of earth. It is not unusual to plant other crops like beans and chili peppers in the same *milpa* ("MIL-pa"), Spanish for a field of corn. In the highlands the farmer's cottage is often set in the middle of the *milpa*, an ancient tradition that goes back to the earliest Mayan communities.

In the lowlands, finding a regular supply of water cannot be taken for granted. When it does rain, depressions in the land become swampy, but these *bajos* ("BAA-hos") can dry out completely. Farmers in the lowlands also practice a slash-and-burn system of agriculture, which involves cutting down a section of forest toward the end of the year, when it is dry, and setting it on fire. A small hole is made in the ash that remains, and the corn seed is then planted. This can be repeated the following year, but after that the ash soil is depleted of nutrients and a

new section of the forest must be burned. Even in the highlands the fields cannot be used indefinitely and there comes a time when the soil must be left fallow for a number of years. A farmer requires experience and skill to know when and where to farm. Slash-and-burn agriculture remains one of the factors accounting for the destruction of the country's rainforests.

INDIAN HOMES

Traditional Indian homes are remarkably similar in design to those of the ancient Maya. The roof is usually thatched, or sometimes tiled, and the walls are made of adobe or cornstalks. Walls are sometimes covered with a lime-based plaster—only the more affluent villager can afford to build a home out of concrete blocks or have a corrugated iron roof. There are usually no windows and the earthen floors are covered with mats made from rushes and reeds or palm leaves. The kitchen area is often little more than a small fireplace made of stones in a corner of the room. Chimneys are not built; the smoke finds its own exit through the roof tiles or eaves.

Above: **A traditional Indian dwelling. The walls are made of cornstalks and the roof is thatched.**

Opposite: **A subsistence farmer carefully tends his corn crop. Corn is the staple food crop of the Guatemalan population.**

An Indian farmer's plot of land is called a milpa *and it is an important part of an Indian's identity. Being a* milpero *("mill-PEAR-o"), a small farmer, is an essential aspect of identifying oneself as a Maya.*

Areas set slightly apart are sometimes used for cooking and this keeps the smoke away from the living quarters. The *temaxcal* ("tem-ASS-cal"), a traditional steam bath that dates back to pre-Columbian times, is sometimes also found situated a short distance away from the home.

Domestic practices, such as the making of sandals from the hides of animals and the fiber of vegetables, still continue, and although machines for grinding corn are becoming more common, it is still not unusual to find women using stone tools for this purpose.

Nearly every home will have some kind of religious shrine, which often takes the form of a statue or a painting of a saint set on a small ledge or table decorated with colored cloth and candles. The sacrifice of animals to honor the gods, which in ancient Mayan times extended to human sacrifices, is still practiced among the Quiché Indians.

HUMAN RIGHTS

Among the Latin American countries Guatemala has one of the poorest human rights records. Between the 1960s and the 1990s the number of Guatemalans who died at the hands of paramilitary death squads alone is estimated at 80,000. Armed guerrillas fighting to overthrow the government of the day represent only a very small percentage of this figure. Most of the victims were innocent civilians, mostly Indians, whose villages were attacked as potential hiding places for guerrillas.

If someone was suspected of being politically opposed to the government, their family was likely to "disappear." The most graphic account of this systematic abuse of human rights is to be found in Rigoberta Menchú's book *I, Rigoberta Menchú*. Trade union leaders and academics critical of government policy were frequently murdered, and even though the long years of fighting are finally over, it is still the case that critics of the

INDIAN MARKET DAYS

Every village normally has one market day each week. Besides serving economic needs, this weekly market performs a valuable social function. People come from a wide surrounding area to shop, sell surplus food or homemade crafts, meet friends, and gossip. Sometimes a party atmosphere develops the night before market day and people drink to the sound of marimba music. Unless a bus service is available, Indians will often spend hours traveling on foot across mountain tracks to their nearest village market, as even the cost of a mule is prohibitively high for many. Whatever is brought to or taken from the market has to be transported home by hand so it is common to see Indian men traveling with a wooden rucksack supported by a sling suspended from a leather band tied around the forehead. Women carry goods in baskets balanced on a cloth on top of their heads.

Market day in an Indian village displays both the traditional past and a more brash commercial culture. Goods like sandals, baskets, and hammocks are displayed and sold alongside canned food, inexpensive perfume, and costume jewelry of varying quality.

Hand-crafted goods often form an important part of the village economy. Mats are used in every home, so there is always a demand for these, and baskets are almost as essential. Baskets are made either without handles, as Indian women balance their baskets on their heads, or with handles for ladinos. Other common items found on sale in village markets are bags and nets made from a string that comes from the agave plant. Pottery, in the form of plates and cooking pots, is another common handicraft, shaped without a wheel and fired in the open air.

ARMADILLOS AND CHEWING GUM

In Petén, Indians supplement their meager income by climbing to the top of sapodilla trees which can grow to a height of 65 feet (20 m). The sweet sapodilla fruit is eaten when ripe, but the immature fruit contains a milky latex, chicle, used in the manufacture of chewing gum. The Indians climb to the top and work their way down, cutting into the bark with their machetes. The sap is collected at the bottom of the tree and sold.

Another source of income for the Indians is the armadillo. Relatively common in the Petén rainforest, armadillos are hunted by Indians and either sold to restaurants or cooked at home. The brilliantly colored guacamaya or scarlet macaw, an endangered bird, is also hunted as its flesh is a highly regarded food.

government have to be careful about what they say. A United States government survey of human rights reported in 1996 that there was a significant improvement in the general human rights situation but confirmed that problems still remain in many areas.

One area of human rights that has seen some improvement concerns the street children in Guatemala City. Some 5,000 children with no families or homes roam the streets of the capital, living lives of petty crime. On more than one occasion small groups of these children have been kidnapped and killed by unknown men who are thought by many to be connected with the police.

MACHISMO AND MARRIAGE

Machismo, from the Spanish *macho* ("MACH-o") for male, means a show of masculinity. Across Central America it remains a recognizable aspect of cultural life as a whole. It is not frowned upon and ridiculed, as in some parts of the world, because equality between the sexes is not taken for granted. A man's traditional role is that of head of the family—by tradition he literally builds the home—and a woman's role is that of mother and homekeeper.

People tend to marry when fairly young, between the ages of 16 and 19, and different Indian regions have their own traditional beliefs concerning the choice of a marriage partner. Some fathers with a son of marriageable age will employ a go-between to find a suitable daughter-in-law. When a betrothal is confirmed, an ox may be killed to celebrate the event. Another feast follows the marriage itself and the festivities may last for many days. The groom's family is expected to bear the cost of this feast as well as other expenses connected with the wedding.

A Guatemalan bride celebrates her marriage. Marriage is an important social occasion and divorce is not common.

67

GUATEMALA'S LIFESTYLE STATISTICS

Physicians	1 per 2,356 persons
Hospital Beds	1 per 602 persons
Televisions	1 per 21 persons
Radios	1 per 25 persons
Telephones	1 per 46 persons
Divorce Rate	0.2 per 1000 persons
Birth Rate	36 per 1000 (the world average is 26)

The usual custom is for the newlywed couple to live with the groom's parents. In rural areas it is not uncommon for the bride's family to receive some small gift from the groom's family as a symbolic "exchange" for the daughter. In the past, if the marriage did not work out, the bride price would be returned and the relationship dissolved.

Also in the past, the marriage ceremony would always take place in the presence of the village *shaman* ("SHAH-muhn"), but nowadays many people have either a civil or church ceremony or dispense with ceremony altogether. Whatever degree of ceremony takes place, it is unusual for rings to be exchanged.

Among both ladinos and Indians it is not common for people to marry outside of their own communities. Parental approval is expected before an engagement is confirmed, and by tradition, the parents of the intended groom make a formal request to the parents of the intended bride. Divorce is very uncommon.

EDUCATION

Six years of primary school are followed by six years of secondary education, which is divided into three years of general studies and three years devoted to vocational studies. The last three years of secondary school lead to examinations that also prepare students for higher education through entry to a university or other institutions of higher learning.

Ladinos have an advantage in the Guatemalan educational system, as the medium of instruction in the majority of schools is Spanish.

In practice, unfortunately, the education system is not available to everyone. Less than half the children of primary school age actually attend school; as a consequence the illiteracy rate is very high. At least half the adult population cannot read or write.

Among the Indian population the illiteracy rate rises to around 75%; it is even higher for Indian women. One reason for non-attendance at primary school is that many parents need their children to work on the farms. Another reason is that Spanish is generally the medium of instruction, which poses a major challenge for Indian children who often speak only their own language.

In recent years there have been successful attempts by Indians to set up their own schools using their own languages. And, although places at university tend to favor the wealthy, the number of Indians benefiting from a university education is increasing. In 1976 there were only about 30 Indian university students in the whole country, but today there are well over 500.

RELIGION

THE FRANCISCAN AND DOMINICAN FRIARS that came with the Spanish armies were not armed, but in their own way they were soldiers, intent on defeating a paganism that they saw as the enemy. Mayan temples and holy books were destroyed and the practice of traditional beliefs was systematically outlawed and suppressed. Indians were forced into Catholicism and those who resisted were punished. Despite this, traditional beliefs were not eradicated, and often Indians managed to observe Catholic rituals, while actually practicing forms of pagan worship. The Christian cross, for instance, was readily accepted as it was already part of the Mayan religion as a symbol of the four directions: north, south, east, and west.

Even today, although most Guatemalans are Catholics, Church ceremonies are often conducted in a way that fits in with traditional Mayan religious thought. This synthesis has been called folk Catholicism and it allows for an element of ancestor worship that is central to Mayan religion but alien to Catholicism.

Above: **Religious icons and inscriptions are sold to hang on the walls of Guatemalan homes.**

Opposite: **Traditional religious architecture and local art combine to give this church a striking facade. In many cases Indian beliefs have been incorporated into the rituals of the Catholic Church to create a unique hybrid, referred to as folk Catholicism.**

ROMAN CATHOLICISM

Roman Catholicism has had a mixed history in Guatemala. It was central to the Spanish colonization of the country, but in the second half of the 19th century, various liberal governments passed a number of anticlerical measures that meant the Church as an institution was severely weakened. In the 1950s and 1960s, however, the Church's fortunes improved as the government valued Catholicism's stance on anti-communism. In the 1970s there were only about 500 priests in the country, a far smaller number in proportion to the population than many other Latin American countries.

Around this time a number of priests were influenced by liberation theology and began to speak up on behalf of the Indians and social equality. Some priests were ordered to leave the country, and in the early 1980s, around a dozen priests were murdered by right-wing military groups. Today Roman Catholicism in Guatemala is losing ground to evangelical Protestantism.

EVANGELICAL CHURCHES

Protestant missionaries were invited to Guatemala by the country's president in the late 19th century as part of the liberal movement against Catholicism. It was the 1950s before the religion began to make inroads into the urban ladino population. By 1983 it claimed to have reached over 20% of the population.

General Efraín Ríos Montt, a fundamentalist Christian who was only president for one year in the 1980s, decisively influenced the growth of evangelism in Guatemala. Under his rule, rural villages were encouraged to form defense militias; those that did not participate became key targets for government attacks. It became clear that one way to avoid becoming a victim of the military was to join an evangelical church so this was what thousands of Guatemalan peasants proceeded to do. Today it is estimated

that about half the country's population has converted to evangelical worship and that by the end of the century it is likely that only about one-third of Guatemalans will be mainstream Catholics.

ANCIENT BELIEFS

The centuries of religious persecution that the ancient Maya suffered at the hands of Spanish Christians did not manage to completely eradicate traditional beliefs. Early religious observances were incorporated into the Catholic religion, and many of today's Guatemalan Indians still adhere to a mixture of mainstream Christianity and pre-Columbian notions of witchcraft and magic. Important stages in a person's life between, and including, birth and death, are marked by ancient non-Christian ceremonies. Indian farmers in more traditional communities not only still use the 260-day Mayan calendar to help decide when to plant corn seeds but chant prayers and leave devotional offerings in the hope of ensuring a good season's growth.

Above: **Evangelical missionaries are often responsible for programs designed to help the local population improve their living conditions.**

Opposite: **Icons of the traditional Catholic faith are still revered. They are always present during religious festivals.**

Rather than a place of somber reflection, the local church is an important part of the daily lives of Guatemalans.

The preservation of traditional Mayan religion alongside the official embrace of Catholicism is apparent in the animist beliefs that many Guatemalans still adhere to and firmly believe in. While Christians believe only humans have a living soul, animism acknowledges a soul in animals, plants, natural phenomena, and even inanimate objects. This is why Indians still worship and pray at various holy places in the mountains that are dedicated to local spirits.

MAYAN RELIGION

It is believed that the Maya thought in terms of long cycles of creation and destruction, with notions of both a heaven and an underworld. Little is known, however, about their gods except that there were a large number of them. Various gods were worshiped by particular sections of the population so that there was, for example, a god for beekeepers, one for hunters, even one for comedians. Whether the Maya held one god to be a supreme creator of all life is a matter of some dispute. There is evidence

SHAMANS

Indians believe in supernatural powers. They also believe that holy people, called shamans, are capable of reaching and interceding with these powers. Shamans, more popularly known as witchdoctors, act as medicine men, magicians, and priests. An Indian who is stricken with an illness is just as likely to consult a shaman as a physician, and there is a wealth of folk knowledge regarding ways of treating illnesses by placating the spirit responsible for the misfortune. At the birth of a child the presence of a shaman is often considered as vital as the attendance of a midwife. The shaman also attends and officiates at marriage ceremonies and at funerals. At the cemetery the shaman turns the coffin around in different directions to fool any evil spirits that might be in attendance. A traditional Indian farmer also consults a shaman before embarking on a new planting cycle.

Most, though not all, shamans are men and they have their own costumes and carry a small bag containing bits of mirror and pottery, red beans, or corn kernels, and other implements used in making prophecies. Some shamans still use the ancient Mayan calendar when calculating propitious days.

to credit Hunab Ku, or Itzamná, with this role, but others argue that these deities are two versions of the same god who was only given this omnipotent role as a result of Christianity being imposed on Mayan culture. Itzamná does seem to be the most important deity. He is typically portrayed as an aged, toothless figure with a Roman nose and reptilian features.

Maya belief conceived the earth, heaven, and underworld to be parts of one unified whole. There were 13 levels to heaven, nine to the underworld, which was called *xibalba* ("shee-bahl-BAH"), and they all acted in accordance with astrological laws that were derived from the study of astronomy. Caves were treated as sacred places, entrances to xibalba, and were richly decorated with glyphs and murals.

There was a Mayan clergy, and the priests were the ones who conducted ritual sacrifices of humans at special times strictly calculated according to the complex Mayan calendar. Slaves and prisoners were common sacrificial victims, along with illegitimate children and orphans. Animals were also sacrificed to the gods.

In Mayan culture there was a religious element to their understanding of time. In the Mayan calendar each section of time, a day for example,

The name of the god Itzamná translates as "iguana house," and this is why he was often represented as having reptilian characteristics.

An incense burner used during religious celebrations by the Maya. This statue was discovered in one of the temples at Tikal.

was envisaged as temporarily belonging to a divine figure who "carried" that period of time until it was passed onto another god. This applied not only to days but also to years, centuries, and even longer blocks of time. This created a never-ending cycle whereby gods could influence life through their rule over particular periods of time.

POPOL VUH

The *Popol Vuh* ("poh-POL VOO"), in the form that it has survived, is an incomplete but very impressive account of Mayan religious thought. It was translated from Mayan into Latin sometime in the 16th century by Indian priests who had been taught Spanish and Latin by Dominican friars. Its existence was not discovered for almost 150 years. Eventually a Spanish missionary discovered the text. He chose not to destroy it but copied it instead and made a translation into Spanish. His copy is the one that has survived and remains a vital source of information about Mayan religion.

The Popol Vuh, which has been translated into over 40 languages, ends with the arrival of the Spanish and begins with the story of how the gods tried, but failed, to make people, first out of earth and then wood. The wooden beings did not melt in water like the earth beings, but their inability to think or to thank the gods resulted in their destruction. Eventually the gods succeeded in creating human beings by using corn to make flesh. They then mixed it with water to form blood.

In a metaphorical sense traditional Indians still see themselves as "Men of Maize," the title of a famous novel by Guatemalan writer Miguel Ángel Asturias. Posters appeared after the 1976 earthquake depicting a single ear of corn and the slogan *"Hombre de maís, levantate!"* (Man of corn, arise!)

COFRADÍAS

Cofradías ("coh-frah-THEE-ass") are religious brotherhoods of lay members. They began as brotherhoods of Indians, established by the Spanish, whose primary responsibility was the welfare of the image of the community's saint. On the day of a religious festival it was the duty of the *cofradías* to carry the saint's image, often a thinly disguised pagan god re-christened with the name of a Christian saint. Toward the end of the 19th century the Catholic Church was more or less closed down for more than 10 years following the expulsion of the Archbishop of Guatemala. People still worshiped, however, and the gap created by the lack of clergy was filled by *cofradías*, even though they had been outlawed in an 1872 presidential

A religious parade led by a local *cofradías*. The banner is carried to identify the brotherhood, followed by a religious float.

Saintly images and statues are the responsibility of the *cofradiás*. They are elaborately adorned and carried through the streets in displays of religious devotion.

decree. The brotherhoods are no longer illegal and are still devoted to the particular saint of their community. During religious festivals members of the *cofradías* take pride of place at the head of the procession.

The chief *cofrade* holds a very prestigious position within the village community, and like all the members of the brotherhood, is elected on an annual basis. He only attains his position after many years of service that gain him the respect and trust of the local community.

New members usually join as teenagers, carrying out civic duties such as keeping the village square clean, and gradually progress through different stages of responsibility and position within the brotherhood according to their age. Women sometimes operate their own *cofradías,* but more commonly they join with their husbands and progress through the ranks of the brotherhood alongside them.

SEMANA SANTA

Semana Santa ("seh-MA-na SAN-ta") is Spanish for Holy Week, the week before Easter, and it is the occasion for some of the country's most important religious celebrations. A procession on the Sunday before Easter, known as Palm Sunday and marking Christ's entry into Jerusalem, begins a week of devotion that culminates on Good Friday with a major procession marking the occasion of Christ's crucifixion. Easter Sunday, two days later, celebrates the belief that Christ rose from the dead, and this day ranks with Christmas Day in terms of joyful celebration.

ST. MAXIMÓN

The worship of St. Maximón in Santiago Atitlán illustrates the fusion of Catholicism and Maya paganism in Guatemala. The image of the saint, dressed in Western clothes, is the focus of a procession during Holy Week, the only time in the year when his effigy is paraded in public. Alcohol is poured over the image by worshipers, and it is customary to blow cigar smoke around him. The religious devotion associated with St. Maximón is, however, very sincere.

His other names include Judas Iscariot and Pedro de Alvarado, the Spanish conquistador who conquered Guatemala, and he is also associated with the ancient Mayan god Mam. After Holy Week it is the duty of a member of the *cofradía*—a different one each year—to house the saint in his home. Visitors who wish to see him are expected to bring some rum and cigars or cigarettes as a gift.

The statues of saints that are carried in procession during *Semana Santa* are reverently dressed in Indian costumes, another example of the interesting way in which orthodox Christianity merges with more traditional beliefs.

Antigua, the original capital, witnessed the earliest *Semana Santa* celebrations in the late 17th century after they were first introduced by Alvarado. When the capital was shifted to Guatemala City, following the 1773 earthquake that destroyed much of Antigua, it was also decided that all the unbroken religious art be moved. This caused a great deal of consternation among the local *cofradías* who removed a number of statues and kept them hidden. Some of the statues that are proudly carried today in Antigua's *Semana Santa* processions date back to the 17th century and are said to be the very ones that were spirited away after the earthquake.

LANGUAGE

SPANISH, THE OFFICIAL LANGUAGE of Guatemala, is spoken by about 60% of the population, while different Indian dialects, numbering over 20, account for the remaining 40%. When the Spanish arrived in the 16th century the predominant Mayan language was called Cholan, which was related to the Yucatec language of the Yucatán peninsula. Cholan is the ancestral language of the Indian dialects that are used in Guatemala today.

The Indian dialect spoken by a Guatemalan functions as the speaker's most important indicator of ethnic identity. In the past, Indians were identified by a combination of dress and language, but nowadays it is the use of their mother tongue alone that shows they still see themselves as Indians.

Above and opposite: **English is not uncommon, but a knowledge of Spanish is important in Guatemala. Spanish is the official language of the country.**

Spanish is spoken by all ladinos, while a growing number of Indians speak both Spanish and an Indian language. In the highlands it is not uncommon for ladino residents to have some acquaintance with the local Indian dialect, but it is rare for a ladino to be able to speak the two languages fluently. Generally, more Indians than ladinos are bilingual. This is partly because the main medium of instruction in schools is Spanish, which means Indians learn it as their second language. Indian languages are not taught in schools in ladino areas and an educated ladino would learn English as a second language. Another way in which Indians, especially males, become bilingual is through their place of work. Outside of Indian villages most employment for men in towns and cities will require the use of Spanish. Finally, there is also the influence of compulsory military service for males. Indian men called up for military service find themselves having to understand and use Spanish.

SPANISH

The Spanish language was brought to Guatemala by the Spanish invaders in the 16th century, and the Spanish clergy taught the language to the Indians to facilitate the task of converting the local population to Christianity. A similar process took place across most of Central and South America. Although the basic vocabulary and grammar of Latin American Spanish is identical to that of modern Spanish, there are differences in pronunciation. The most obvious difference in pronunciation is the absence of the soft "s" found in European Spanish.

Both Latin American and European Spanish are relatively easy languages to pronounce, with the stress generally going on the penultimate syllable. Words that end in the letters "r," "d," "l," and "z," unless there is an accent, have the stress on the last syllable.

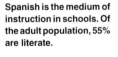

Spanish is the medium of instruction in schools. Of the adult population, 55% are literate.

The word *gringo* is derived from *griego* ("gree-A-go"), the Spanish word for Greek, and it has come to mean any non-local person in general and a North American or European in particular. There was a time when the word was used, especially in Mexico, in an unkind and often insulting way, but nowadays the term is used in a neutral way to simply indicate a tourist or visitor.

ANCIENT MAYA

The writing system of the ancient Maya mostly survived in the form of inscriptions on stone. Only four Mayan books have survived the ravages of time. The importance of writing, however, is shown by the fact that the god who may have been the supreme spiritual force, Itzamná, was also considered the inventor of writing.

Most Mayan writing has now been deciphered, but there is still some uncertainty as to the linguistic nature of many of the 1,500 glyphs that make up the written language. Mayan glyphs consist of a central symbol with various additions placed around, or even within, the central symbol. It is generally agreed that most glyphs contained a phonetic value, and while this means that the symbols give some indication of how they were pronounced, it remains unlikely that it will ever be known what the language actually sounded like. At the same time the glyphs also contain an ideographic element, an ideogram being a character that represents an idea, and this feature of the writing has been more successfully interpreted by historians and linguists. This means that even though the language cannot be spoken, the meanings contained in the ideograms allow it to be read and translated.

Inscriptions in stone have left a lasting record of the ancient Mayan language.

ANCIENT WRITING

Apart from inscriptions on stone, the only original examples of the Mayan language are found in four ancient manuscripts. The text appears on long strips of paper called codices, made from the pulverized bark of fig trees, that measure less than 10 inches (25 cm) across but several yards in length. The length allowed each strip of paper to be folded back-to-back, concertina-like, and pictures of books on pottery show that the folded pages were covered with jaguar skin.

The Maya wrote with brushes and pens made from turkey feathers, and their writing was exuberantly colored with paints made from vegetables and minerals.

MODERN MAYA

The various Indian dialects spoken in Guatemala are distributed geographically, with the greatest variety occurring in the western half of the country. The Quichéan peoples who live in the midwestern highlands make up the largest group of Indian speakers.

The Academy of Mayan Languages was founded in 1986 with the intention of preserving and encouraging Mayan literacy. It conducts literacy programs for Indians across the whole of Guatemala and has helped to develop a uniform Mayan alphabet for the various Indian languages. Its council is composed of representatives from each of the 21 Mayan language groups, and one of its on-going tasks is the compilation of dictionaries for each of the languages.

ARAWAKAN LANGUAGES

Arawakan is a family of over 50 South American languages, many of which are still spoken today, with a small residue in Guatemala due to the presence of the garifuna. They were once common and were spoken as far north as Florida and as far south as the border between Argentina and Paraguay. It was the first Indian language heard by the Spanish when they landed in the Americas, and to it we owe the words "canoe," "tobacco," and "maize."

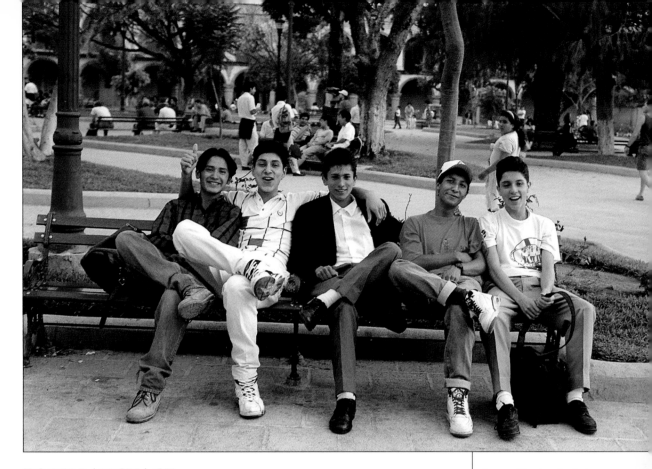

BODY LANGUAGE

Generally body language is more common and noticeable in urban areas than in the countryside. In both environments, however, direct pointing with the hand is unusual partly because the hands are used for aggressively rude and offensive expressions. This is not unique to Guatemalan society; it is fairly common across Latin America. If there is a need to point toward someone it is more likely to be accomplished by pursing the lips in the direction of the person being indicated. In order to call someone over, the hand is held out and then waved downward and toward the body. This is considered rather overt but acceptable. In order to attract someone's attention in a more discreet manner a "tssst" sound is made in the direction of the person being signaled.

When it comes to courting, young couples are generally conservative and open displays of hugging or kissing are not common. This is especially true in rural areas where holding hands is likely to be the most obvious display of a relationship.

Among friends, physical contact is common. Hand gestures are used to emphasize a point or to attract attention.

ARTS

THE TALENT AND RESOURCEFULNESS of Guatemalan culture finds expression in a variety of art forms. The artistic skill of the ancient Maya is evident in the architecture of temples and palaces, though there is little reason to think this was their only field of artistic endeavor. Ancient architecture, however, has survived the passing centuries and remains the most visible demonstration of Mayan creativity. The ruins of Uaxactun in Petén bear testimony to late Pre-Classic architecture, but the Classic site of Tikal is the most important site of Mayan architecture.

Contemporary Guatemalan culture expresses itself in literature and folk art such as weaving and dressmaking. Weaving goes back to pre-Columbian times when vegetable fibers were used as thread and insects and minerals were used as dyes. No examples have survived, but depictions of dress on the frescos and relief sculptures of Mayan buildings show that ancient Mayan dress was similar to that produced today.

Left: **Carved religious statues stand beside images of an ancient Indian heritage.**

Opposite: **Bright colors and a dramatic landscape make this wall mural the perfect backdrop for a photograph.**

Stelae like this one were used by the Maya to record significant events. They can be found around temples, usually near a plaza or open courtyard.

ART IN STONE

It is with stone, more than any other material, that Mayan art finds its grandest and most compelling expression. Huge pyramid temples were constructed using limestone blocks over a core mound of rubble. They were built without the help of wheels or metal tools and yet were constructed in such a way that they were sufficiently aligned to allow sophisticated and accurate astronomical observations. Large, single-story palaces containing many rooms were built, but judging by their uncomfortably small size, it is possible the elite lived elsewhere and the palaces were reserved only for special occasions.

In Classic times the temples and palaces were always built around a large plaza, and around this large courtyard, rows of stone slabs, or stelae, were placed. These stone pillars were richly illustrated, usually with a male figure in some form of ceremonial dress, and recorded important dates such as those of a royal accession or birthday.

The ruins of Tikal, one of the largest Mayan cities and ceremonial centers, are located in the rainforest of Petén. Tikal was first occupied around 600 B.C., but its grandeur dates to the Classic period (A.D. 300–900). By the 10th century Tikal had been mysteriously abandoned. It was between A.D. 600 and 800 that the great pyramids, palaces, and plazas were built. The most important buildings, ceremonial in nature, occupy an area of about one square mile (2.6 square km), but excavations have revealed a surrounding area of about six square miles (15.5 square km) that contained smaller residential buildings.

TIKAL

The center of ancient Tikal is a great plaza occupying an area of about two acres. To the north of the plaza stand rows of stelae. At the east end stands the Temple of the Great Jaguar, christened Temple I by archeologists, which contained the tomb of an 8th century Tikal ruler whose name translates as Lord Chocolate. To the west is Temple II, which may contain the as yet undiscovered tomb of Lord Chocolate's wife. North of the plaza is a structure known as the North Acropolis, which contains temples and a maze of interconnecting stairways and passages. Excavations have revealed two giant masks and a burial chamber where a ruler was buried along with nine servants, a crocodile, and turtles.

South of the plaza are a ball court and a large, four-acre site known as the Central Acropolis, which contains a number of palaces. To the west of the Central Acropolis are two more temples including Temple IV, one of the tallest buildings ever constructed by a Native American culture.

The great temples and pyramids are astonishing when one considers they were built without the benefit of wheels or draft animals to transport the massive stone blocks, some weighing as much as 60 tons, that needed to be quarried and placed in position.

Relief carvings adorned temple walls and ceremonial items such as thrones. They give a striking impression of the features of the people and the clothes and jewelry they wore.

MAYAN ART FORMS

The skill and artistry of the Maya appear not only in the construction of large temples and palaces but also on a smaller scale in low-relief carving, in which the design stands out from the surface. Mayan artists perfected this art form on their stelae and on temple panels.

Pottery was painted in fine detail, and it was common to fire the clay at relatively low temperatures in order to achieve the desired colors. This reduced the working life of the vessel, but the artistic effect was considered more important. Mayan pottery originating around A.D. 700 is regarded as some of the finest pottery produced in ancient times. Surprisingly, the potter's wheel was not known to the Mayan world.

The single most precious material for Mayan artists was jade. Fine, low-relief carving was carefully inscribed onto jade surfaces using tiny chisels and cane drills. Many examples of jade jewelry have been found in Mayan tombs. Jade was also inlaid in shells and stone and even in a person's teeth as a mark of social superiority.

MAYAN LITERATURE

The four original Mayan texts that have survived are all concerned with religious matters, and calendrical and astronomical calculations like lunar eclipses and the cycles of Venus. Spanish sources describe Mayan writings on history, myth, and science, and it is very likely that a rich literature has been lost forever, partly due to the zeal with which Spanish priests destroyed Mayan books on the grounds that they were pagan propaganda. Inscriptions on stone mostly relate to records of various rulers and their families; these also reflect the common Mayan concern with calculating exact dates.

A secondary source of Mayan literature exists because Spanish missionaries taught their language to some Indians who used it to translate their own writings into Spanish. This is how the famous *Popol Vuh* managed to survive.

TEXTILE ARTS

The woven cloth produced in the highlands represents an art form in itself, even though the finished material is made for everyday use. Although machine-manufactured garments are becoming increasingly common, many garments are still made in village homes using a backstrap loom. The loom consists of a wooden board with vertical sticks around which the lengthwise strands, or warp, is wound. The crosswise thread, the woof, is passed through the loom and fastened in place by a handle that allows every other warp strand to be lifted. The technology is simple, yet it allows intricate and brightly colored patterns to be woven into the garment. Later, other patterns may be embroidered on the cloth to add more color and complexity to the final product. The traditional blouses, *huipils*, are made by sewing together two or more pieces of hand-loomed cloth.

A fascinating aspect of Mayan temples is the way in which the buildings, or parts of the building complex, were aligned so as to facilitate celestial observations. On a certain day a particular part of a temple, usually a door or window, would be aligned to provide a view of a star or planet in an especially auspicious position.

The backstrap loom, used by Guatemalan women to produce brightly colored fabrics.

The backstrap loom is traditionally used only by women, while men use foot looms. The foot loom, which was introduced by the Spanish, permits the weaving of larger pieces of cloth. Foot pedals, connected to the sticks that control the warp and rollers, are used to feed the thread and collect it. The woof strands are fed by way of wooden handles that are operated manually.

MUSIC

Music has always been central to Mayan culture; there are many references to singing and the playing of flutes in the *Popol Vuh*. The most common traditional instrument used in Guatemala is the marimba, which is very similar to a vibraphone. It was introduced into the Caribbean from Africa via the slave trade and is now popular across Latin America.

The marimba was originally played using gourds of varying sizes to produce different notes. The modern marimba has its own double keyboard and wooden tubes to resonate the sounds. At festival time a

traveling marimba orchestra, complete with brass accompaniment, usually arrives on the back of an open truck in any village that cannot muster its own team of musicians. Towns are more likely to have their own resident orchestra.

Indians have other instruments for ceremonial occasions. During religious processions the *chirimía* ("cher-er-MIA"), a flute-like instrument, is often used. It produces a sad tone somewhat similar to the oboe. Various types of drums are used, often simply made by tightening the skin of an animal over a suitably shaped piece of wood. Rhythm is also provided by shaking gourds filled with beans or seeds.

DANCE

Dance is an essential accompaniment to most festivals where the dances are often fairly unstructured. The dances are usually performed only by men, who dress up for the occasion in elaborate padded costumes, hideous masks, elaborate wigs, and plumed hats. Such costumes have to

The marimba produces a melodic sound, and in conjunction with other instruments, is an important part of any Guatemalan celebration. Traveling bands play to appreciative audiences all over the country.

be hired, and the choice of dance often depends on how much money the village can afford to spend for a set of costumes. The dances themselves may last for hours; they have sometimes been compared to endurance marathons because, toward the end, the exhausted and tired dancers are often barely able to stay on their feet.

More structured dances, requiring practice, take place in the more traditional Indian towns including Todos Santos and Chichicastenango. A common dance, the Dance of the Conquest, reenacts the encounter between the Spanish and the Maya. Dancers representing the Spanish wear masks painted to represent the pale skin of the Europeans, with large, white noses attached. The dance, first choreographed by a Spanish priest in 1542, climaxes with the victory of the Spanish, but nowadays Indians enjoy the spectacle with little regard for its symbolism.

Another dance, the Dance of the Volcanoes, also celebrates a Spanish military victory over rebellious Indians that took place near the volcano Agua in 1526. The Quiché Indians have their own dance, known as the Dance of the Black Ones, dedicated primarily to a black figure known as Elk, or the Black One.

WRITERS

In recent decades Guatemala has produced two Nobel Prize winners for literature: Miguel Ángel Asturias in 1967 and Rigoberta Menchú in 1992. In their work both writers have discussed their country's plight and politics. Menchú's book, *I, Rigoberta Menchú,* tells the heart-rending and true story of how the Indians suffered at the hands of the military authorities. The novels of Asturias, who was born in 1899, contain a mystical strand as well as social protest on behalf of the Maya. He has been called the inventor of magical realism, a term used to describe a genre of South American literature characterized by this fusion of the real and the surreal. As a young writer he lived in Paris where he was greatly influenced by surrealism and where he translated the *Popol Vuh.* His first important book, translated into English as *Legends of Guatemala,* was about the cultural life of the Maya before the Spanish arrived. After his return to Guatemala he wrote his major novels, beginning with *The President* in 1946 and then *Men of Maize* in 1949, considered his most important novel. *Men of Maize* concerns itself with the terrible plight of the Indian peasants. Asturias went on to write an epic trilogy about the exploitation of the Indians by the United Fruit Company on their banana plantations. He died in 1974.

Rigoberta Menchú was born in Guatemala in 1959. By the age of 8 she was working in a coffee plantation and saw her brother die of malnutrition. At the age of 20 another of her brothers was murdered by the army and her father died a short while later. Her father was a member of a group

Above: **Miguel Ángel Asturias.**

Opposite: **Lighting fireworks in preparation for the Dance of the Conquest.**

peacefully occupying the Spanish Embassy in the capital when the army set fire to the building. A short while later her mother was kidnapped and murdered by the army. She became a refugee in Mexico, and there she wrote the harrowing story of her life in the book *I, Rigoberta Menchú.* She was awarded the Nobel Prize for literature in 1992 and the Nobel Committee described her work as "A vivid symbol of peace and reconciliation across ethnic, cultural, and social dividing lines." The country's military rulers were upset that she received the Nobel Prize, but Menchú spoke out for peaceful change: "Even though the tortures and kidnappings had done our people a lot of harm, we shouldn't lose faith in change. … Every day the vote against fear is gathering strength and this is the foundation for change in the future."

Another important contemporary writer, Mario Roberto Morales, also writes about the social and political condition of his country. His style of writing is experimental and his most recent work consists of 24 parts that combine nonfiction with fiction. Excerpts from pre-Columbian religious texts and testimonies by contemporary Indians are combined with a story of an Indian boy who is forced to join the army after his father is murdered by the military.

COLONIAL ART

Colonial art in Guatemala is best represented by the old churches and other buildings that the Spanish built in the 16th and 17th centuries. The town of Antigua, the original capital of the Spanish, contains many splendid examples including the ruins of the Cathedral of San José, built in 1680. Originally it was a tremendously impressive building with 18 chapels, five naves, and a huge dome, but a number of earthquakes caused the collapse of its walls. Only two of the chapels have been restored.

Another church, La Merced Church, has survived earthquakes with less damage, and its intricately ornamented facade is one of the best examples of colonial architecture in Guatemala. Antigua has been declared a World Heritage Site, ensuring preservation of the city's rich architecture and the likelihood of conservation funds. Although complete restoration of many buildings is unlikely, preservation of the more important ruins means that colonial architectural styles will remain visible.

Above: The architecture of many buildings in towns like Antigua stands as a legacy to Spanish colonial design.

Opposite: **Nobel Prize winner and social activist, Rigoberta Menchú.**

LEISURE

THE TYPICAL GUATEMALAN works hard throughout the week, resting only on Sunday, and apart from national holidays and the occasional fiesta takes no other holidays. Only a tiny minority of the population can even contemplate a week's vacation or a holiday abroad.

Sunday is an important rest day and, except for street markets, virtually all businesses are closed. People attend a church service in their best clothes in the morning, and the afternoon is spent relaxing with the family.

There is a large divide between the leisure activities of the urban wealthy class in the capital and the rural population. Guatemala City has an entertainment area known as Zone 10 where clubs and discos are located. In rural areas people are more likely to relax by visiting friends.

Above and opposite: **In Guatemala City people take advantage of the many opportunities for sport and leisure. In rural areas there are not as many facilities, and local festivals and celebrations provide most of the entertainment.**

SOCIALIZING

Leisurely socializing is an important aspect of the Guatemalan lifestyle for both Indians and ladinos. People find time during the course of a day to talk and relax informally with friends and acquaintances. Only amongst the small wealthy elite is socializing organized around dinner parties or cocktail gatherings. Market days are especially important occasions for people to meet up with acquaintances on a regular basis and this is as true for the traders as for the shoppers. Two traders may be side by side in a village square with their stalls selling identical goods but they are often more interested in socializing with each other than competing for a sale.

Village festivals also serve a vital social function by bringing together family members who may otherwise be working in different parts of the country. Even festivals with a religious origin serve a larger social purpose

Festivals provide the chance to relax, dress up, and socialize.

because they provide one of the few opportunities for people to escape the world of work. The nights before a festival are often convivial occasions when people mix and mingle over drinks and dance to a live marimba orchestra.

In urban areas young people, especially ladinos, socialize in a way that is not very different from their contemporaries in North American towns and cities. From about the age of 14 young people have their own social groups, and leisure time is spent going out to eat together or visiting the local cinema. In the rural areas there are fewer opportunities to socialize during the week, but Sunday provides a day of rest and relaxation when young people meet together.

BALL GAMES

The passion that many Guatemalans have for ball games such as soccer and basketball may well have ancestral origins. The most popular game among the ancient Maya seems to have been *pok-a-tok*, a team game for which special ball courts were built. The game involved trying to place a rubber or stone ball through a ring placed just above the players' level on the wall of the court. The rules forbade touching the ball with either hands or feet, and it had to be bounced off other parts of the body. Players wore protective padding and while the stakes were often very high in terms of cash and property, there was also an element of fun because it was traditional for the winning team to claim the clothes of any spectators who were slow enough to be caught when the game was over. More alarmingly, there is reason to believe that losing players were sometimes sacrificed.

SOCCER

Sports are an important leisure activity for young Guatemalans. Soccer is the single most popular sport, and the media always cover important matches. There is a professional soccer league, and each season there is growing excitement as the better teams play one another in their struggle to become the league champions.

Soccer matches, especially important ones held in Olympic City in the capital, are noisy but cheerful events. Letting off firecrackers is a traditional way to express jubilation following a victory. Most spectators stand up to watch a game. Refreshments are sold during the match by vendors who carry large coolers full of beer, dispensed into small plastic bags and drunk with a straw.

Soccer is not taught in schools in the way that baseball, for example, is taught in schools in the United States, but it is always featured as one of the options in physical education classes for boys. It is rare for a girl or woman to play soccer. At school, girls play basketball and volleyball.

Soccer is enjoyed in many forms. The national league is closely followed by most Guatemalans, and many young boys dream of playing professionally.

Preparations for a day at the lake begin early. Buses transport people and supplies from the towns and villages.

LAKESIDE LEISURE

The picturesque Lake Amatitlán is about 10 miles (16 km) south of Guatemala City and has become a favorite destination for people who want to escape city life on weekends. Buses depart from the capital regularly—as many as five an hour—and are usually crowded with families who bring picnics. They are unperturbed by the presence of Pacaya, an active volcano on the southern slopes of the lake. At night people like to watch the color effects around the cone of the mountain as it bubbles away and produces an orange glow in the night sky.

During the day the lakeside area is crowded with families. Boat trips across the lake are very popular, but unfortunately much of the water in the lake has been polluted so swimming is usually confined to special areas where the water is kept clean.

The ancient Maya celebrated the summer solstice—the time when the sun is farthest north of the equator—by coming to the lake to bathe and to pray at an altar in a nearby forest. Rituals designed to placate the gods

and ensure a good harvest included sacrificing children in the lake. These days, in early May, the lakeside area is the site for a wide range of leisure activities including dancing, live music, and water sports. Special decorated boxes, filled with sweets, are sold for the occasion.

DANCING AND MUSIC

Sophisticated young Guatemalans love to dance. In the nightclubs of Guatemala City the most popular forms of dancing are salsa and disco. Salsa is a type of music as well as a dance, combining Latin jazz with rock music to produce a fast and energetic rhythm ideally suited to the disco floor. Discos are not usually found outside the capital; in smaller towns and rural areas, dance and music is often confined to festivals. Religious holidays are the occasion for displays of traditional dance in traditional costume, the most common dance being the *Baile de la Conquista* ("BY-leh day la con-QUIS-ta"), the Dance of the Conquest, which dramatizes the defeat of the Indians and pokes fun at the Spanish.

FESTIVALS

COUNTLESS FESTIVALS TAKE PLACE in Guatemala, and while most of them have a religious foundation, there is also an emphasis on social relaxation and enjoyment. The week before Lent, traditionally a period of abstinence and restraint, is often the occasion for a carnival in ladino communities. The week before Easter is the most important time for festivals, even more important than Christmas. It is a time when most Guatemalans hope to return to their own villages and celebrate with their families. Some aspects of the religious festivals reveal the unique way in which traditional Mayan beliefs have merged with Catholicism.

Above: **Young Indian boys wait their turn to ride the carousel. In rural areas traveling shows often accompany festival celebrations.**

Opposite: **Father and son, dressed as Romans, take part in an Easter parade. Most festivals in Guatemala are religious.**

FIESTAS

The Spanish word for a party or festival, *fiesta* ("fee-EST-a"), has entered the English language with the same meaning. Just about every village and town in Guatemala has at least one day in each year devoted to a particular saint, although the anniversary celebrations frequently extend to cover a period of several weeks. In urban ladino areas, the days of a fiesta are characterized by religious processions accompanied by musicians playing in the street. Sometimes a local beauty contest takes place.

In areas where Indians form a majority, a fiesta merges with more traditional pre-Columbian forms of celebration. Participants, traditionally dressed, dance and celebrate in a more exuberant way than elsewhere. In the town of Rabinal, for example, dance dramas that reenact ancient Mayan festivities are performed. Wherever a fiesta takes place, though, a party atmosphere prevails at night as fireworks light up the sky with color. More food and drink is consumed than at any other time of the year.

CHICHICASTENANGO'S FIESTA

The town of Chichicastenango is renowned for its Indian character. The annual fiesta celebrating St. Thomas on December 21 is one of the most spectacular festivals in Guatemala. As many as 10,000 Indians participate in the celebrations. For three days there is a succession of parades through the narrow streets, headed by Indians from Chichicastenango wearing their traditional dress woven from black wool and richly embroidered with Mayan symbols.

Traditional dances lasting many hours also take place, and a special pole is erected around which ritual dances are performed. In the dance known as *Palo Volador* ("PAH-lo vo-la-DOR") men tied by a rope to the top of a 65-foot (20 m) pole unwind the rope and descend through the air to the ground.

The festivities form an important part of the daily life of the community. As is the case throughout the country, the parades and dances provide participants with opportunities to meet with one another and socialize. On the morning of St. Thomas' Day all babies born in the previous year are communally christened at the village church. At night the air is alive with the color and sound of fireworks.

SEMANA SANTA

Easter's *Semana Santa* ("seh-MA-na SAN-ta"), or Holy Week, is the most important occasion for religious festivals in Guatemala. Holy Week is characterized by huge, colorful processions, the use of giant floats on which devotional statues of saints are carried aloft, and the liberal use of incense. In some of the larger towns with more extravagant processions—Antigua being the most famous in this respect—the larger floats weigh as much as three tons and require a team of 60 or more men to carry them.

Different village communities have their own ways of celebrating the significance of Holy Week. In the village of Chiantla, in the western highlands, there is an unusual blending of the holy and the profane that revolves around the idea of the Apostles escaping from the Good Friday procession and hiding in the countryside. There follows a mock hunt until eventually all the Apostles are escorted back to the procession. The character of Judas, the apostle who betrayed Christ to the authorities, is often represented by a scarecrow subjected to mocking and insults before

During Holy Week processions are common. Statues of Christ are displayed to commemorate his crucifixion. Bright costumes and flowers add to the color.

The Thursday before Easter is the only day in the year that Indians deliberately avoid eating corn. Special deliveries of bread are made and the bread is eaten in commemoration of Christ's meal at the Last Supper.

being put on trial and burned for his act of betrayal. Sometimes the scarecrow is dragged through the streets on a rope attached to a donkey.

The days of Holy Week itself tend to follow a familiar pattern from one year to the next. Wednesday is usually market day when villagers buy sufficient supplies of food and flowers for the occasion. The following two days are devoted to religious processions. On the evening of Good Friday, after a commemoration of the act of crucifixion, the Christ figure is returned to the church. Saturday is a quieter occasion for people to relax and enjoy themselves. Church services are held on Easter Sunday.

The week before Holy Week, known as *Semana de Dolores* ("seh-MA-na day doll-ORE-ez"), is a busy time of preparation, when churches and the village as a whole are swept clean and decorated with a variety of flowers and colored streamers. The costumes that dress the holy images are removed for cleaning and repair, and rehearsals are scheduled for the coming processions and parades.

CHRISTMAS

For Christians, the celebration of the birth of Christ cannot be anything but a major religious festival, but Christmas takes second place to *Semana Santa* in terms of public celebration and spectacle. One reason may be that Easter, marking as it does spring's arrival and winter's end, resonates with ancient Mayan fertility rites in a way that Christmas does not. It is only in ladino towns that one part of the Christmas story, the search for lodgings by Mary and Joseph, is reenacted. Known as *las posadas* ("las po-SAH-das"), Spanish for a shelter or lodging, it takes place over the nine evenings leading up to December 25. Christmas in Guatemala has none of the commercial overtones it has acquired in North America and Europe. The vast majority of the population is too short of money to buy presents.

ANTIGUA'S ALFOMBRAS

The city of Antigua is famous for the splendor of its *Semana Santa*, not least because of the *alfombras* ("al-FOM-bras")—Spanish for carpet—made of sawdust and flower petals. The main street of the procession and the area outside the church are carpeted with elaborate patterns made out of sawdust and petals, and when the procession is over, some people collect pieces of the *alfombras*, believing they now carry miraculous properties.

Alfrombras are made all over Guatemala at festival time, but the people of Antigua seem determined to maintain their exemplary reputation in this field of endeavor. More than 200 people work through the night, creating the main religious pictures and patterns, and individual households create their own *alfrombras* outside their houses if the procession is passing their way. The Procession of the Roman Soldiers takes place in the early hours of the day before Good Friday, when participants run through the streets announcing Christ's death penalty and are followed by men on horseback representing the Roman army. When the festival is over the results of everyone's labor are swept away.

Huge kites fill the sky on All Souls' Day. Getting them aloft requires a team effort. They are believed to relieve the suffering of souls not yet admitted to heaven.

ALL SAINTS' AND ALL SOULS' DAYS

November 1 is All Saints' Day and November 2 is All Souls' Day, also known as the Day of the Dead. Both days are celebrated across Guatemala and some towns are famous for their fiestas at these times. Although both days are religious festivals, they are usually celebrated with parties.

In the small town of Santiago Sacatepéquez, the townspeople construct huge paper and bamboo kites in preparation for the Day of the Dead. On November 2 the kites are released as a way of encouraging the release of dead souls suffering in purgatory. The kites can measure as much as 20 feet (6 m) across and it requires a team effort to get them airborne. Any town with the name of Todos Santos, or All Saints, could be expected to make a special effort on All Saints' Day, and people flock to this town from the surrounding countryside for the famous horse races that take place. The festival begins with a stampede of horses across a large field. On the following day the cemetery becomes the focus of prayers and rituals designed to assuage the souls of the dead.

THE ESQUIPULAS PILGRIMAGE

Esquipulas, a small town east of the capital and close to the border with Honduras and El Salvador, attracts thousands of devotees from all over Central America for a festival on January 15. The focus of prayer is a statue of Christ carved from a block of balsam and placed inside the church in 1595. One legend has it that the statue was inspired by a vision of a black Christ appearing to local Indians, although in reality the Spanish chose a dark wood for the statue in the hope that a dark-skinned Christ would help convert the Indians. Esquipulas had been the site of religious ceremonies before the Spanish arrived and the Maya had more than one black deity.

Villages in Guatemala choose at least one person from their community to represent them at the festival. Thousands more arrive on foot. On January 15 enormous lines form outside the church as devotees wait for their chance to light a devotional candle at the statue, which is believed to possess miraculous powers, a legend that developed after the Bishop of Guatemala claimed to have been cured of an illness in 1737.

Lighting candles is the culmination of the pilgrimage undertaken by many Guatemalans each year. The Esquipulas Pilgrimage is a solemn occasion, given over to prayer and religious devotion.

Corn plays an important role in the life and legends of the Guatemalan people. More than a staple food, it is considered in Indian mythology to be the source of humanity.

CORN FESTIVALS

In a land where the successful planting and harvesting of corn is crucial to people's livelihoods, it is not surprising that ceremonies and festivals are associated with corn. Before planting takes place, special masses are held in the local church. On the night before the first seeds are planted, incense is often burned in the fields and candles lit in homes. The following morning the candles are placed in the fields, and after sowing, a celebratory meal takes place. The first seeds are traditionally sown by the oldest member of the family.

The planting season occupies the months of March and April. The months from October to December are devoted to corn harvesting when further celebrations take place. During harvesting an important task is the selection of seeds for the next planting cycle. In some villages, particularly large ears of corn are tied to the side of a rocket and fired into the sky. If all goes well and the rocket soars to a great height, this is taken as a good omen. Fireworks are employed again when processions carry the harvested corn back to the village and another celebratory feast marks the happy occasion.

CEREMONY OF THE EIGHT MONKEYS

One of the Mayan calendars is based on a cycle of 260 days, composed of 13 smaller cycles of 20 days each. The 261st day is the Mayan New Year day. The New Year is celebrated in a festival known as the Ceremony of the Eight Monkeys. The village of Momostenango in the western highlands is famous for its observance of this ancient ceremony. Originally a pagan festival, it has now merged with Catholicism, and celebrations begin with a church service on the eve of the New Year.

At dawn the next day, villagers make their way to a hill a short distance away where altar mounds are located. These mounds measure between three and 10 feet high and offerings of broken pottery are placed on top of the mounds. Behind each altar stands a shaman who receives the offerings on behalf of the gods. Each Indian making an offering makes a request to the gods and the shaman burns wafers of sacred incense to accompany the request. This ceremony continues until dusk and then moves to another holy site nearby where the shamans pray and burn incense throughout the night.

Momostenango means "the place of the altars," and as the town's name existed long before the Spanish arrived, this is proof of just how ancient the ceremony is.

FOOD

THE BASIC CROP that has been essential to life in Guatemala for centuries is corn. Beans and squash are also important; without these three crops most Guatemalans could not survive. For many Indians beans provide a good source of protein and they are eaten with corn tortillas ("tor-TEE-yahs") almost daily. Meat is too expensive for many people and is often consumed only on special occasions. In rural areas people produce most of what they eat. Food that does need to be purchased is often paid for from the proceeds of other crops, such as vegetables, grown primarily for their cash value.

In urban areas there is more variety in the type of dishes available. Guacamole, made from mashed avocados and onions, is popular as are rolls made from steamed corn dough and filled with beans or a small amount of meat. Other foods such as pork chops, grilled chicken, and hamburgers are also available to those who can afford them. The most popular inexpensive dish is beans served with rice. It usually features as a standard item in *comedors*. A *comedor* ("com-e-DOR") is an eating establishment similar in style to a café serving inexpensive food. There is usually no menu because local people simply know, or ask, what is available. In larger towns and cities there are restaurants as well as *comedors*, but in villages the main places where most people eat are in the two or three *comedors* that are always found close to the main market.

A typically large breakfast at home consists of eggs, beans, and tortillas, sometimes accompanied by a sour cream sauce. Breakfast in the highlands may also feature a bowl of *mosh* ("MOSH"), a mixture of oats and milk. For most families the main meal of the day is eaten at lunch, and though beans may be included, once again it is the tortilla that forms the basis of the meal. Bananas are often eaten with meals.

Above: **Picadillo, a popular Guatemalan dish.**

Opposite: **Bananas and corn are both prepared in a number of ways, but one or the other is usually present in most meals.**

FAST FOOD, GUATEMALAN STYLE

In the cities there are the internationally familiar fast food establishments found in so many parts of the world. If they are not as common as in North American cities, it is mainly because the majority of people cannot afford to eat this way.

Affordable fast food in Guatemala takes a different form and is very much geared towards people who are traveling. Migrating for work is a common phenomenon and this, combined with the prohibitive cost of private transportation, means that buses are usually very full. When the buses make a stop, especially in the busier transport hubs, street vendors appear out of nowhere with a range of fast food items and drinks. They crowd around the open windows of buses offering quick snacks as well as a variety of complete meals.

The most common fast food snack is the *tamal* ("TAM-al"), made from boiled cornmeal and wrapped in a banana leaf. Stuffed peppers are another favorite.

TORTILLAS AND BEANS

Tortillas and beans are the traditional staples of the daily meal for the average Guatemalan. Tortillas are thin, circular pancakes made from corn and are usually just topped with beans and other vegetables, or turned over to form a type of sandwich with beans inside. They may be seasoned with chili salsa or just plain salt. In rural areas they are freshly made early each morning, but machine-made tortillas are becoming more common, especially in towns. They need to retain their moisture in order to taste wholesome, so are frequently kept wrapped in a slightly wet cloth for this reason. Sometimes, though, tortillas are dried out by being toasted when they are still fresh; they then retain a crisp tastiness.

Beans cooked in different ways—fried or boiled—are often eaten with tortillas, but they also make a delicious meal on their own when cooked with chilis. When eaten with tortillas, they are boiled until soft and then mashed into a paste, which is then refried. The other method of preparing beans is to boil them and serve them hot in their own juice.

For most Guatemalans tortillas are considered the bread of life. Made from corn, no meal is considered complete without this bread.

Chilis add color and spice to most Guatemalan dishes.

CHILIS

In the *Popol Vuh* chilis, made by the gods out of corn, are named as a food enjoyed by the first people. They have kept their popularity ever since. A bowl of chilis, raw or pickled, always appears on a restaurant table.

A tremendous variety of chilis is available and an essential element in the colorful displays of food that grace any Guatemalan market day are small and large mounds of red and green chili peppers. They are bought to make various sauces that may be added to most meals, and their versatility allows for a lot of variety in the taste of the sauce.

Various tastes are possible, due not only to the different sizes and colors of the peppers, but also to how they are cooked. Generally the longer chilis are cooked, the more intense the taste. Many restaurants in Guatemala include a guide to how hot each dish is according to the amount of chilis it contains. If a symbol of a man with fire exploding from his mouth and ears appears beside the name of a dish the diner can be certain it will contain the hottest chili available to the cook.

TORTILLAS

This recipe will make about a dozen tortillas, best enjoyed piping hot immediately after cooking. The chief ingredient, *masa harina*, is corn mixed with lime water and ground into a fine meal. A tortilla press, readily available in stores selling Mexican food, is almost essential because it takes a lot of practice to shape them by hand with the same success as a Guatemalan.

2 cups *masa harina*
8 fl oz (225 ml) water
1 teaspoon salt

Mix and stir the *masa harina*, water, and salt in a bowl. Knead gently by hand until the dough is firm and not falling apart in your hands. Shape the dough into a dozen balls of equal size and place each ball into the tortilla press. The press produces a tortilla ready for frying over medium heat on each side for about one minute. Eat as soon as possible after frying.

Soft drinks known the world over are also popular refreshments in Guatemala.

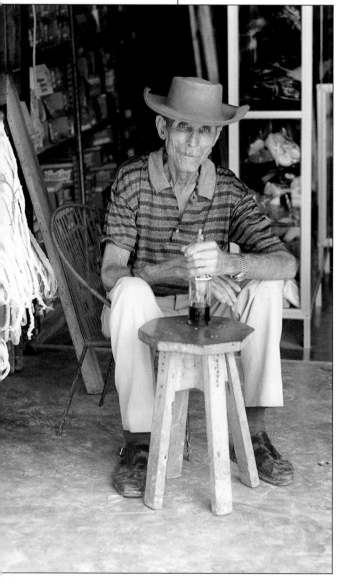

DRINKS

The most popular non-alcoholic drinks are coffee and cocoa. Coffee is usually drunk with sugar and is surprisingly weak considering the quality of the coffee produced on the large plantations.

Tea is also popular, usually without milk, and there are a number of fresh fruit and vegetable juices available. In the highlands a warm but watery drink is made from corn or rice, flavored with sugar, honey, cardamom, or even powdered chili.

Beer was introduced to Guatemala in the late 19th century by German immigrants, who came to the country to grow coffee. It is now very popular across the country. There are two main brands of lager whose names translate into "goat" and "rooster."

Aguardiente ("ag-wahr-de-EN-tay") is a strong drink made from sugarcane. It is popularly known as "White Eye." Indians sometimes pour a small amount of it over the statue of the saint they are praying to. Along with *ron* ("RON"), or rum, this is the most common strong alcoholic beverage. There are different types of rum available; the less expensive brands are sometimes mixed with soft drinks, partly to disguise the poor taste.

NON-INDIAN CUISINE

Ladino culture has influenced Guatemalan food, although the contribution is by no means merely Spanish in character. The rich tastes of Mexican cuisine are also evident. Hamburgers and steak, favorite meals in the United States and Europe, are increasingly popular in towns and cities. Indeed a ladino meal without meat is almost as uncommon as an Indian meal with meat.

One of the more famous Guatemalan regional dishes is chicken served in a spicy sauce made from pumpkins. In recent years a dish called *chao mein* ("CHOW MANE") has become popular with ladinos. Although it does consist of vegetables and rice, there is little other resemblance to the famous Chinese dish of the same name.

It is mainly in the cities, and Guatemala City in particular, that one would find a variety of food styles other than the traditional Indian dishes. In rural areas and smaller towns it is uncommon to find much change from the corn- and vegetable-based diet of the Indian population, though some interesting regional variations do occur.

Ancient Mayan rulers enjoyed meals topped with chocolate sauce made from cocoa beans. The sheer extravagance of this is best appreciated when one realizes that the common people at that time used cocoa beans as a form of currency.

TOO GOOD

The story from the *Popol Vuh* has already been told of how the gods finally made humans out of corn after early prototypes failed using first mud and then wood as raw materials. When they finally succeeded, using corn, another unexpected problem arose. People made from corn surpassed the gods' expectations, because of the excellence of the raw material. The corn people were so good that they came dangerously close to being gods themselves. They could see too far and understand too much. The creators, therefore, had no choice but to "blow a mist" into their eyes so that their vision and understanding were blurred.

QUICK NOTES

OFFICIAL NAME
Republic of Guatemala

HEAD OF STATE
The president, currently Alvaro Arzú Irigoyen

AREA
Total land area is 40,536 square miles (104,988 square km)

POPULATION
10,998,602 (1995 estimate)
15,827,000 (estimate for 2010)

CAPITAL
Guatemala City

MAIN TOWNS
Quezaltenango, Antigua, Chichicastenango

HIGHEST POINT
Mount Tajumulco, 13,845 feet (4,218 m)

RAINFALL
Average annual rainfall: 52 inches (132 cm)

LANGUAGE
Spanish is the official language, but there are 20 different indigenous languages spoken by 40% of the population

MAJOR EXPORTS
Coffee, sugar, bananas, cardamom, cotton, beans, and legumes

MAJOR IMPORTS
Petroleum (for generating electricity), machinery, consumer goods

LITERACY
Adult population: 55% (male 63%; female 47%)

RELIGION
Roman Catholicism (which among Indians often includes aspects of their pagan past and is known as folk Catholicism) and Protestantism (mostly evangelical and fundamentalist)

CURRENCY
Guatemalan quetzal, divided into 100 centavos
7 quetzals = US$1

LITERATURE
In recent decades Guatemala has produced two winners of the Nobel Prize for Literature: Miguel Ángel Asturias (1899–1974) in 1967 and Rigoberta Menchú (1954–) in 1992

MAJOR FESTIVALS AND HOLIDAYS
Semana Santa (Holy Week): week before Easter
Labor Day: May 1
Independence Day: September 15
Columbus Day: October 12
Revolution Day: October 20
All Saints' Day: November 1
All Souls' Day: November 2
Christmas: December 25

GLOSSARY

aguardiente ("ag-wahr-de-EN-tay")
A strong drink made from sugarcane.

alfombras ("al-FOM-bras")
Spanish for carpet; used to describe the street carpet made using sawdust and flower petals during Holy Week celebrations.

cofradías ("coh-frah-THEE-ass")
Religious brotherhoods composed of lay members.

comedor ("com-e-DOR")
An eating establishment similar to a café and serving inexpensive, basic food.

fiesta ("fee-EST-a")
A party, festival.

glyph ("GLIF")
A sculptured symbol or character.

huipil ("WEE-pil")
Overblouse or tunic, worn tucked into a skirt.

ladino ("lah-DEE-no")
People of mixed Spanish-Indian ancestry.

ladinization
Term describing the growing influence of ladino (Western) lifestyle on Indian culture.

milpa ("MIL-pa")
An Indian farmer's plot of land, used mainly for the growing of corn.

mosh ("MOSH")
Porridge-like mixture of oats and milk that is eaten for breakfast in the highlands.

Popol Vuh ("poh-POL VOO")
An ancient Mayan text written by Indians that has survived in the form of a Spanish translation.

Semana Santa ("seh-MA-na SAN-ta")
Holy Week, the most important occasion for religious festivals in Guatemala.

Shamans ("SHAH-muhns")
Holy people, or priests, considered capable of reaching and interceding with supernatural powers.

stela ("STEEL-a")
Archeological term referring to an upright pillar, usually inscribed for commemorative purposes.

tamal ("TAM-al")
A popular snack made from cornmeal and boiled after being wrapped in a banana leaf.

Tikal
One of the largest Mayan cities and ceremonial centers, located in the Petén rainforest.

tortillas ("tor-TEE-yahs")
Thin circular corn pancakes, the primary staple in the diet of Guatemalan Indians.

traje ("TRAH-hay")
Traditional dress.

BIBLIOGRAPHY

Everton, Macduff. *The Modern Maya*. Albuquerque: University of New Mexico Press, 1991.

Coe, Michael. *The Maya*. London: Thames & Hudson, third edition, 1984.

Janson, Thor. *In the Land of Green Lightning*. California: Pomegranate Artbooks, 1990.

Menchú, Rigoberta. *I, Rigoberta Menchú: An Indian Woman in Guatemala*. New York: Verso, 1984.

Morris, Walter (text) and Fox, Jeffrey (photographs). *Living Maya*. New York: Harry N. Abrams, 1987.

National Geographic. Washington DC: The National Geographic Society, Vol. 146, No. 5 (Nov. '74); Vol. 173, No. 6 (Jun. '88); Vol. 182, No. 5 (Nov. '92); Vol. 183, No. 2 (Feb. '93).

Tedlock, D. (translator). *Popul Vuh*. Simon & Schuster, 1985.

INDEX

INDEX

INDEX

names, 55
National Advancement Party (PAN), 29
National Congress, 30
Nobel Prize winners, 95–6

Osorio, Colonel Arana 27, 31, 33

Pacific Ocean, 7, 11, 12, 37
per capita income, 40
Petén, 10, 11, 15, 16, 20, 30, 37, 44, 45, 55, 60, 66, 87, 88
pok-a-tok, 100
police, 29, 33
political opposition, 34
political parties, 29, 30, 35
political supression, 34–5
ponchito, 50
Popol Vuh, 76, 91, 92, 95, 118, 121
population statistics, 7, 10, 11, 47, 48, 53–5, 58, 59, 60, 68, 69, 72, 73, 81
poverty, 3, 55, 58, 59
president, 30, 31
Puerto Barrios, 42

quetzal, 17, 35, 52
Quezaltenango, 13

rainfall, 10, 12
rainforest, 10, 14–16, 37, 39, 45, 55, 63
refugees, 15, 55
restaurants, 115, 118
Revolution of 1944, 26
rivers:
    Cuilco, 8
    Motagua, 8
rural life, 60–1

saints, 79, 105–107, 110
Santiago Atitlán, 49, 52, 79
Santo Tomás de Castilla, 38
Semana Santa, 78–9, 107–9

shamans, 68, 75, 113
slash-and-burn, 11, 15, 55, 62–3
slavery, 32, 51, 54, 75, 92
snacks, 116
soccer, 100, 101
Sololá, 50
Spanish conquest, 11, 13, 22–3, 32, 47, 49, 51, 71, 79, 82, 94
Spanish descent, 53–4
Spanish influence, 19, 49, 50, 57, 97
Spanish missionaries, 20, 24, 71, 76, 82, 94
stelae, 22, 88
street children, 66
sugarcane, 11, 37, 38
Supreme Court of Justice, 30

tamal, 116
textiles, 38, 49, 91
Tikal, 20, 21, 44, 76, 87, 88–9
Tikal National Park, 45
tortillas, 115, 117, 119
tourism, 11, 15, 43–5
trade unions, 34, 64
trading partners, 38
transportation, 60, 116

Uaxactun, 87
Ubico, Jorge, 26
Umánd, Tecún, 32
unemployment, 37, 39
United Fruit Company (UFC), 26, 27, 42–3, 55, 95
United Nations, 29, 35
United Provinces of Central America, 25
universal suffrage, 30, 31
university, 69
United States, 26, 27, 32, 35, 38, 39, 42, 51, 55, 58, 66

volcanoes, 7, 8, 11, 94, 102
volleyball, 101

wealth distribution, 3, 57, 58, 59
weaving, 49, 87, 91–2
women, 57, 60–1, 67–8, 69
workforce, 37, 39, 59
World War II, 41

xibalba, 75

PICTURE CREDITS
Camera Press: 1, 29, 31, 58, 73, 77, 78, 79, 95, 96, 107, 110
DDB Stock Photo: 8, 17, 39, 42, 44, 60, 88, 90, 103
Focus Team–Italy: 115, 119
Guatemala Tourist Commission: 13
ANA Press Agency: 74, 86
Hutchison Library: 14, 61, 76, 93
North Wind Picture Archives: 23, 24, 32
Harry S. Pariser: 21, 83
David Simson: 6, 18, 28, 33, 36, 46, 54, 67, 69, 71, 80, 81, 82, 85, 98, 101, 111, 114, 117, 118, 120, 123
South American Pictures: 3, 5, 10, 16, 19, 37, 41, 47, 50, 53, 56, 57, 62, 63, 65, 66, 70, 87, 89, 92, 97, 99, 100, 104, 106, 109, 112
Sue Cunningham Photographic: 38, 45, 49, 116
Sylvia Cordaiy Photo Library: 7, 102
Nik Wheeler: 4, 52, 72, 94, 105